Embrace Your Life

Robins Compere

Copyright © 2018 by Robins Compere. All rights reserved.
No part of this book may be reproduced or utilized in any form or by any means, electronic or mechanical, including photocopying, recording, or by any information storage or retrieval, without permission in writing from the publisher except in the case of brief quotations embodied in critical reviews and certain other noncommercial uses permitted by copyright law.
For permissions requests, write to the publisher, addressed "Attention: Permissions Manager," at the address below.
Ordering Information: Quantity sales–Special discounts are available on quantity purchases by corporations, associations, and others. For details, contact the Special Sales Department at the address below.

Publisher: Robins Compere
Address: 2002 B Longleaf Dr.
Birmingham, Alabama 35216
Web Address: https://www.facebook.com/Embrace-Your-Life
Telephone: (256) 457-1664

Library of Congress Control Number: 2018902037
Embrace Your Life–Non-Fiction–Haiti & US

ISBN: 978-0-692-05764-3
Printed in the United States of America

Embrace Your Life

Robins Compere

Robins Compere

Dedication

To the God of my life. To the best parents in the world who raised me.

My mother, Marie Suzette, who gave me everything she had of value in her life,
and my father, Zachari, who worked two to three jobs in the United States of America for over 40 years so that my siblings and I may have an education and a means to provide for our families.

To my lovely wife and friend, LaQueena, who supports all my endeavors, even when she disagrees with me.

To my sisters, Rose, Rodeline, and Frandeline, along with their beautiful children, Gia, Lilly, Elijah, Sarina, and Elora.

Robins Compere

Table of Contents

Preface 9
Prologue.. 12
Chapter 1: The Plight of Children in the World............................... 17
Chapter 2: My Father's Childhood in Haiti 22
Chapter 3: My Mother's Childhood in Haiti 32
Chapter 4: My Interesting Childhood in Haiti.................................. 45
Chapter 5: Other Interesting Childhood Stories 68
Chapter 6: Joseph's Interesting Childhood....................................... 84
Chapter 7: Embrace Your Children Equally 98
Chapter 8: Politics Create Dysfunctional Homes............................. 115
Chapter 9: Embracing Life Even in Prison....................................... 130
Chapter 10: How Do We Embrace Our Life?................................... 136
Chapter 11: How I Embrace My Life in the United States............ 143
Epilogue... 170
Prayer 178
About the Author... 180
Resources... 181

Robins Compere

Preface

Embrace your life is a piece that God inspired me to write as I began to reflect on billions of children that are growing up in dysfunctional homes around the world. Those poor children are usually the bearer of great prophecy, scientific gifts, natural healing abilities, and are natural geniuses who are possibly destined to invent mindboggling strategies to save the planet from disease, poverty, racism, systematic deception, destruction, and violence. As a teacher, I see children every day who look great and jovial in public, but who may not particularly be happy and safe at home. While I may not be privy to the kind of life they are living at home, I know for a fact that almost one hundred percent of the children I see on a day-to-day basis always seem to be happy and very courteous.

Most of them say "Bonjour" to me with a smile on their face, but I know that sometimes a smile is nothing short of a façade. Children have an innate ability to mask their true feelings, hurt, and disappointments in their young and promising life. They instinctively learn to adapt to the unavoidable tumultuous changes that families go through in our fast-paced society. The same is true even for children who are orphaned, and who do not know if they will have a meal. Children learn to cope with grief and pain early in life. Unfortunately, we as adults put them in situations to deal with pain as early as when we entrust them into the arms of strangers at a daycare facility.

I remember vividly the first day I dropped off my daughter, Robyn, at a private school daycare in Birmingham. She cried so much that I almost wept like a big baby. In fact, I sat in a room a few steps away from where she sat bawling. I was still able to hear the childcare providers working hard to console her. Quite frankly, I simply did not cry, because I was too embarrassed to do so.

I left the facility feeling horrible for leaving my only child, at the time, to good people who were still strangers meeting Robyn for the first time. They took great care of my daughter; they loved her and she ended up loving them. Still, leaving her there was not easy.

The first month, dropping her off was unbearably dreadful and depressing. She used to cry every morning when we approached the building, even before I dropped her off. She eventually accepted her fate and coped with her situation, which is what most children do after a few weeks of daycare.

Reflecting on my daughter's difficulty to embrace a new reality encouraged me to be the teacher who shows his students an enjoyable time when they come to class. I thought that there was a slight possibility I might be the only person positioned to make them happy for the day. I embrace my life as a teacher and a guide. I commit to do the best that I can while I still have the blessed opportunity, privilege, and honor to teach and lead them, as they will be the next leaders of the world.

While teaching the French language to students, I work hard to be one of the best memories they have about their childhood. I do not want to be the only person who is encouraged to embrace life and do what I can to bring happy memories to children. That is why I decided to write this book with a purpose in mind.

The purpose of this book is to encourage readers to embrace their life no matter the circumstances in which they grew up, no matter the mistakes they have made in their childhood, and no matter the betrayal and the loneliness they have experienced as a child. No matter what their current situations may be at home, at work, at church, at the hospital, in prison, or anywhere else, I want readers to be encouraged and to know that when they embrace their life, they make a difference in the world by impacting another individual's life.

While I was praying, researching, and preparing myself to write my inspiration, I realized that part of embracing life no matter the circumstances is to acknowledge that the author of life wrote both the introduction and the conclusion of our existence. I find the same to be true for even those of us who grew up in dysfunctional homes.

Whoever God may be, if He planned for us to be here, there must also be a calculated plan and purpose for each one of us.

Prologue

Whether one believes and accepts the Bible as a holy book, or rejects it as a work of fiction for shallow thinkers and gullible individuals prone to believe anything blindly, most of us will agree that throughout the ages, many children were raised in dysfunctional homes. Christians who truly read their Bible find it replete with stories of dysfunctional "godly" families where there were favoritisms, animosities between siblings, rivalries between husbands and wives, deception, envy, and even murder.

A few such examples can be found in books like Genesis, where we read about the very first biblical family torn apart by jealousy and envy. A deadly fight between two brothers claimed the life of the youngest, and caused the exile of the oldest. Further, in the book of Genesis, the father, Abram, put his first son, Ishmael, out of his house because his wife, Sarah, wanted her son, Isaac, to be the only legitimate son in the house, who was the rightful heir of Abram's wealth. Sarah no longer wanted to argue with a rival woman who lived under the same roof and who would compete against her for her husband's attention.

The Bible says that Ishmael almost died of thirst crossing the wilderness. The child's own father subjected him to death by dehydration and starvation in the long run.

Similar stories include the strife between Jacob and his twin brother, Esau. Their father loved Esau more than he loved Jacob, and vice versa. Their mother loved Jacob more than she loved Esau. Although neither twin killed the other, they were arch nemesis for years. Jacob lived in the house of his uncle for a while and was tricked into marrying two sisters.

In books such as first and second Samuel, we find the story of David, who was neglected as just a shepherd boy, and

Samuel, who was born in a home where two wives were rivals, and who antagonized each other for years.

Non-Christians and atheists who do not have the time or the desire to read about biblical dysfunctional families can simply research children's quality of life around the world. In doing so, they will soon be confronted with a harsher reality than that recorded in the biblical narratives.

Whether you are a young adult or older, just take a moment to reflect on your own upbringing and that of some of your classmates or childhood friends. Think of the horrific stories that you have heard. Maybe you were sexually abused growing up, or maybe your parents simply neglected you to pursue their own heart's desires. Maybe you did not have it that bad; you were simply not the favorite child. Perhaps you were the sibling who made life a living hell for a younger one. Perhaps you have survived a childhood of nightmares, neglect, and abuse that you are still reliving in the mental realms even as you read this book.

I want you to know that I have been commissioned to encourage you to embrace your life no matter what you went through growing up. I am positive that you will greatly benefit from this book even if you have never experienced any of the hardships referred to here. Knowledge is power, and you never know when you might need to use the information hidden in this book.

May the Lord bless you and yours as I allow you access to my experiences, and the wisdom that I have acquired from reading and observing God's children, as well as the inspired written word.

In this book, I am going to invite you to reinterpret your life's experiences as a child, or even as a young adult. I intend to show you that it is better to embrace your life no matter the circumstances than to be depressed, suicidal, guilt-ridden, and angry about a past that nobody will ever be able to change, but that everyone who cares, including myself, can certainly use to better your future.

Today I am doing my part in helping you to rebuild your confidence and equip you to use your past as a weapon to defend not only your future, but also that of other children who are currently trapped in horrible family conditions that can potentially ruin their glorious hidden future.

If you will allow me your time and undivided attention, I will share with you my own personal stories and experiences of other children whose stories I heard growing up. I will also use the story of Joseph in the Bible to show you several situations that will encourage you, and even enjoin you to embrace your life no matter your current or past circumstances.

One may ask why would anyone need to be encouraged to embrace or accept his or her life. My answer is that the world is filled with individuals who hate the life that they have been given. Many adults wish they had a different job, life partner, church, bank account, etc. The same is true for many children who find themselves stuck in families or countries who do not protect or want them. Some of them are in homes ill-equipped to raise them properly. Others live in conditions that expose them to harsh situations, or wicked, cunning, and vicious predators.

I heard horrific stories of racist people who purposely go to Haiti to adopt children, and then bring them to the United States simply to make them work. There were other stories of so-called UN peacekeepers who have violated boys and girls. Those children will need our help and guidance when it comes to accepting and embracing life with all its challenges.

I personally know a woman who told me that she hated God growing up. She said that she could not understand why God would put her in such a poor and destitute family. Life was so hard growing up that she was tired of eating the same kind of rice (not literally) every day. She did not like her clothes, and she hated the second-hand toys that were given to her during the Christmas season. She was so poor that one winter when she and her siblings were cold and freezing, her loving and creative mother turned on the oven and left its door open so that the heat could keep them warm.

Her father was not around to help with the bills, as he was young, frivolous, handsome, and too busy marrying other women and bringing other children in the world who would eventually suffer. Today, this woman is a happy mother, and she has two beautiful daughters whom she cares for daily. Her life purpose and goal is to help make the life of children a joyful experience. She understands now why her family was so poor and dysfunctional.

She loves her parents despite her childhood. She forgave them for not attending any of her school events, including her high school graduation. She cares for them dearly, and as much as possible, she helps to provide for their needs.

No one can blame her for feeling the way she felt as a child. Her innocence and curiosity left her wondering and asking many questions like that of other children all around the world. There were no adults available to answer her childhood inquiries, just as many children today go to sleep at night with unanswered questions and missing, or irresponsible parents who set them up for a troublesome and tumultuous childhood.

Come with me as I expose my heart. Pray with me as I attempt to minister to you. God's children living in adult bodies, allow me to persuade you to embrace your life no matter your circumstances. Please allow me to note that this book is also for the children growing up in "functional" families.

What is a functional family? My simplest definition is that a functional family is composed of both parents caring for their children and creating enjoyable memories for them.

I have discovered that our childhood prepares us for our life purpose in adulthood. If you are a child reading this book, I pray that it helps you understand that your family's unfortunate situation will not last forever. I want you to know that there are adults all around the world who pray for you, and who are working hard to make the world a better, safer, and more children-friendly place to live.

Chapter 1
The Plight of Children Around the World

Humanity is a large dysfunctional family. We are all part of the same earthly household, but we act as a typical crazy family plagued with strife, envy, jealousy, and murder. We cannot seem to act righteously toward each other. That is why one part of the family is always protesting to have its civil rights respected, while the other part of the family indifferently ignores his siblings' desperate plea for justice.

As brothers and sisters of different ethnic groups, we sometimes act as if we are not all created equal. Because we have different shapes, sizes and skin tones, we despise each other. Therefore, we exploit and abuse each other instead of helping and teaching each other. We talk about each other and refuse to talk to each other. As a result, our children grow up without fathers and mothers to take care of them. Our actions are analogous to that of childish and selfish siblings who fight over petty issues such as who gets to sit in Daddy's favorite chair, who will hold the remote control, or whose turn it is to ride in the front seat with Mother. Unfortunately, while adults fight over ownership of air spaces, international waters, regime changes, oil reserves, gas, and precious metals, children become casualties in devastating wars. If they survive our wars, they endure economic collapses, which causes some of them to starve, while others become homeless.

In some demographics, many fathers are incarcerated, hospitalized, or dead; leaving single women to raise the next generation. In other demographics, the fathers and mothers are at work eighty percent of the day, while the children are at a daycare. I certainly understand that most of us do not have the choice to stay at home with our children and provide the maternal and paternal care that they need, but we have to admit that our children suffer.

It makes sense why they follow in our footsteps when they become older, and why when we become elders, they put us in adult "daycare" retirement homes. This is not a personal attack or accusation on parents who already detest this way of living, or mothers who already deal with mommy guilt. Rather, I am talking about a systematic deplorable situation where children suffer the most when they leave their homes at 6:30 in the morning, only to return at 6:00 in the evening . . . and sometimes later. To me, that system creates dysfunctional societies in which children are disconnected from their parents, and forced to embrace loneliness and fear as early as the age of four.

Some of us do not put our children in a daycare facility, but we leave them with a family member or a friend to look after them. Sometimes, our friends and family members abuse them. We justifiably neglect our children while trying to provide for them. We expose them, as vulnerable as they are, to individuals who could be mentally unstable and hurt them.

Most of us know that many "civilized" countries of the world, especially the United States of America, have specific laws made to protect the rights of children. Unfortunately, those laws do not guarantee the safety of most children. Every now and then we hear many stories of children that have been molested, raped, physically and psychologically abused, and reduced to nothing. Most of the time, the law catches the perpetrators of violent crimes against children, but sometimes many children are afraid to report such incidents, and consequently, nothing happens to change their unfair and unbelievable living predicament.

I heard the sad story of how, in Birmingham, Alabama in November 2015, an eight-year-old boy was going to be charged with murder. Allegedly, the boy beat an infant to death because the baby refused to stop crying. By now you should be asking yourself the same question I asked myself while watching the news story: Where were the parents of those children? Why were an eight-year-old child and an infant so neglected that murder and prison had to be the final results?

Regrettably, those children represent the millions who are neglected and mistreated, while nothing happens until it is too late. Ninety-nine percent of the time, only the children—not the parents—suffer the long-term, permanent damages.

While I lived in Huntsville, I heard the story of a father who repeatedly raped his daughter. He was only caught because his wife stumbled upon a video recording of his repugnant actions with his own daughter. He was sentenced to many years in prison, but the damage was already done to both his daughter and his wife. He put his family in a very bad predicament to where they are going to need serious counseling to be able to continue living without him.

His daughter may have to battle chronic depression at some point if she does not embrace her life and make the best of what she has left. Her horrible childhood experience can serve as the catalyst for some new laws protecting little girls from their fathers, or her experience could spur new ideas to protect children against sexual and physical abuse by close family members.

If you are a child reading this book, I want to encourage you to speak to your doctor, teacher, pastor, or any responsible adult who will listen to you about any sexual and physical abuse to which you might be subjected, whether at home, church, school or the park. It is important that a responsible adult knows about your suffering so that your psychological therapy and healing may start. Remember, if you live in the United States of America, you are somewhat protected by laws prohibiting adults from hurting you and violating your innocent body. Even if it is possible that no one will believe you, I implore you to share your unfortunate situation with someone who will listen.

Embracing your life does not mean you cannot defend and protect yourself. On the contrary, it means that you do not blame yourself for what someone else did to you. It simply means that you accept your life as it is, while working on improving every facet of it.

In some less-developed nations, where there are no child services to police parents, teachers, and extended family members in the way they treat their children, most children are still being mistreated. They are sometimes sold to slavery, or physically and psychologically abused. Often their own parents subject them to unimaginable atrocities. In some of those countries where human trafficking is pervasive, parents often sell their children into prostitution for material gain.

Imagine living in societies where there are no agencies; no places to protect the rights of children betrayed by their own family members. They have no one to defend their cause. They grow up to become broken adults who, most of the time, perpetuate the vicious cycle of abusing children the same way they were abused (I have provided links at the end of this book as researched and documented proof).

In America, we are used to popular sayings such as "abused people abuse people." Most aggressors come from dysfunctional environments. The fact that children are still being mistreated around the world indicates that some of us adults have not yet accepted and embraced our life no matter the circumstances. We will all be prone to hurt others unless we have been healed from our negative experiences as children.

That explains the reasons some men have a hard time forgiving their father for abandoning them growing up, or physically or sexually abusing them when they were vulnerable. Some women have a hard time forgiving their mother for not believing them when they said that Uncle Doe molested them, or Deacon Toutou was not as saved as he pretended to be. Adults today can only forgive their parents for their mistakes growing up if they embrace their life despite all that happened to them in the past. If you happen to be a son or daughter who is not on good terms with your parents as a result of their neglect while raising you, I want to encourage you to make peace with them as soon as possible, or else you will never heal completely from your past, and thus embrace your life.

Also, if you happen to be a child reading this book in a country where there are no explicit laws to protect you against abuse at home, school and church, I am praying that the Lord will make a way out for you. Meanwhile, you still need to attempt to talk to someone who can potentially help you. Talking about your pain helps to release your burden, and allows someone else to help you with it. If you are an adult living in a country without laws to protect children, consider it your mission to motivate your lawmakers, and try to steer them in that direction. It might be the purpose of your life. You were probably born to protect children and to be the person to make your government set in place laws that guarantee children's safety.

In the following pages, I am going to share with you several stories, including my own, to help you realize that embracing your life no matter the circumstances will be the best decision you will ever make for yourself, your family, and your world. My objective is to help you learn how to embrace your life.

I am delighted to share my parents' childhood stories with you in the first few chapters of this book. Learning about their childhood has motivated me and encouraged me to live life while making the best of my situations. My father's story helped me to realize that I do not have to settle for less, and always position myself for success. My mother's story taught me that with God, I can survive anything in life. I have learned many great lessons from their childhood stories, which have inspired me to go on in life to defeat and go against all odds. Every story in this book has personally blessed me, and I know for a fact that they are going to do the same for you.

Chapter 2
My Father's Childhood in Haiti

My father was born in 1948, in the northern department of Haiti; a little section called Cormier. It was a small commune of Grande Rivière du Nord, which happened to be the birthplace of Jean-Jacques Dessalines, one of the greatest leaders in the Haitian Revolution that led to the 1804 victory. My father was part of a huge family of nine children, but the two oldest died. My father was the fifth child of his parents. Even though both of his parents worked to provide for him and his six other surviving siblings, they were the poorest family in the neighborhood.

They were God-fearing people, in fact, the entire neighborhood consisted of Seventh-day Adventist Believers. My father's mother was named Elnide Compere, and she worked for a young married pastor named Max Charles. The young Zachari was 11 years old when his mother worked away from home. His older brother was already 15 years old, and he had an older sister who was 13.

His mother was a nanny, a housekeeper, and a chef for the Max Charles family. Her job required her to sleep over the pastor's house, leaving her children at home. Sometimes my father's mother spent an entire month with the Charles family before returning to her own, but just for a few days.

His father's name was Francillon. He worked on people's farms, spending entire weeks away from his family. Often, my grandfather would leave his house on Sundays, and would not return until Fridays late at night. He was responsible for caring for two small churches, one of which was a few hundred yards from his house, and the other a few miles away. He was not a pastor, but he was what the Haitians call a "konditkè legliz." He was a church elder who did the work of a pastor.

His duties were to take care of the church business and the church worship service. Part of his job requirements were to ensure that the tithes and offerings went to the Haitian Seventh-day Adventist Mission. My father told me that even if both his parents were working, their earnings were never enough to take care of them. His father literally slaved for the church, but he could barely take care of his seven surviving children. He met the needs of the church and of the poor congregants at the detriment of his own children.

Zachary's grandparents were somewhat financially secured. They had many acres of land upon which they hired farmers to work. They were very generous and good to their grandchildren, and my father enjoyed going to their homes with his siblings.

Because his parents worked away from home on a regular basis, my father, who was not the oldest child, had the duty of watching over the children at home. He had two older siblings, Samuel and Mary, and younger siblings, Enande, Psalmiste, Jean, and Crane. My father assumed the position of a leader in the family.

Zachary loves to joke about his parents being the Haitian "Brady bunch." He said that his parents gave birth to nine children, because they used sex instead of a television set for entertainment, which was understood, because they did not have a TV. It was not a good joke, but I appreciated his sense of humor.

Going to school was always challenging for my father and his siblings. He told me that back in those days, his parents had to pay fifty cents a month for their tuition. It is so unfortunate that children in his days did not have free education. The director of their school, our modern-day principal or head of school, lived far away from the school. His salary was about $100 Haitian dollars per month. The pastor's salary was acceptable and helped him to buy some land and take care of his family.

My father's siblings lived in Cormier, and they had to be at school by seven in the morning. They used to wake up at four in the morning and walk to Grande Rivière to attend school. Imagine waking up extra early to walk two plus hours to get to school. Imagine, as a child, sitting in school after such a long walk. Imagine walking back home for another two hours.

It is sort of depressing reflecting on the plight of children in oppressed countries, and their incredibly challenging educational journeys. My father's childhood was tough, but as he told me his childhood story, I learned that he was a fighter who embraced his situation and made the best out of it. He told me in Haitian Creole, "Depi'm piti, map goumen ak lavi'a." That means, "I have been struggling with life since I was a child."

The school he attended did not provide lunch for the children, therefore my father and his siblings brought with them a few mangoes as their lunch. On the way back from school, they ate more mangoes and oranges from the trees that were along the way. Those children suffered and were malnourished because their parents worked and earned very little. Sometimes my father and his siblings would go to their grandparents' home to have something to eat while their parents were out for the week. My father said that life at his grandparents' home was better than life at his parents' house.

Even though going to school was a challenge, my father would have loved to continue with his education, but he did not have money to continue beyond middle school. Consequently, he dropped out of school and began to find ways to educate himself for his survival. He was fortunate to be introduced to a man at his church who taught him, free of charge, the science of carpentry. That man who taught my dad did not only bless one generation, but the skills he graciously imparted into my dad has helped him to meet the needs of many people of his generation. They have met the needs of people in my generation, and they will meet the needs of my children's generation.

We must remain conscientious of the fact that when we help meet a need, we do not only bless the person that we see, but we bless everyone associated with them. Let us embrace our life and meet the needs of the people we can see, so that we can influence the lives of those that we cannot see.

Once, my father and his older brother, Samuel, were walking and chatting about life. They were on their way to their grandparents' home to get some food for their little siblings. It was one of the many times that they'd heard the rumble of an airplane flying over the area.

Zachary said to his older brother, "One day we will be on an airplane."

His brother responded, "Ou mèt di sa fò," meaning "that is a fact."

They both looked up and believed that they would be a passenger on an airplane. That may seem unimportant to a 21st-century reader who is well acquainted with technology, and who is a frequent flyer, but to my father and uncle, it was a dream that was as big as me saying to one of my sisters while watching a Powerball lottery drawing on television, "You see all this money in America? One day I will be a millionaire."

My father had big dreams. Even if he grew up in a place of poverty with a lack of education and a lack of modernity, his dreams surpassed and outshined his situation.

As my father grew older and his siblings became a little more mature, the family moved from Cormier to Grande Rivière du Nord in search of a better life. My uncle Samuel went to a school for carpentry so that he could have a trade to work and support himself and his family. Meanwhile, my father started transporting sugarcane on his head, walking distances of 20 kilometers, or 12.4 miles, to go sell them at the marketplace to survive and provide for his younger siblings. He did not earn much from his business, but he earned an honest living. He used to buy a load of sugarcane for ten cents, and when he was lucky, he sold it for fifty cents.

When my uncle Samuel left his parents' home and started working at Emballage Adventist in Port-au-Prince, my father was still at home in Grand Rivière trying to provide for his younger siblings, because his father had already passed away. His mother no longer worked for the Charles family, and had begun to sell food such as fruits and vegetables so that she could earn a living for her children. My father grew impatient with his life in the North, and decided that he would attempt to join his brother in Carrefour Port-au-Prince.

Because Zachari had learned how to write and read in elementary school, he used his limited ability to write and put together a letter addressed to Samuel, asking him if he could come live with him in Port-au-Prince so that he could find employment opportunities. Back in those days, Port-au-Prince was the place for Haitians to find employment.

Samuel wrote him back explaining why he could not allow him to come live with him. Samuel responded with another letter saying that what he was earning at the Emballage was not enough for him to pay his bills, and therefore he could not afford to take care of my father. Against my uncle's wishes, my dad decided that he would move to Port-au-Prince anyway, and position himself to benefit from any opportunities to work as a carpenter.

When my father arrived in Port-au-Prince despite his brother's discouraging letter, Samuel asked him to go back to Grande Rivière, because he claimed that he could not take care of him due to a lack of money. His sister, Mary, who also lived in the same house, told my dad to stay and not go back to the countryside. My father told Samuel that he was not going back; that he'd come to stay.

My father had his mind made up that he was going to be successful in Port-au-Prince. He'd arrived motivated and ready to take advantage of any given opportunities that should arise.

My father told me that he was a great and hard worker who was ready to leave a lasting impression on any employer who would dare take a chance on him. He said that as soon as he reached Port-au-Prince and started letting people know of his skills, a family hired him to build a closet. They even gave him a deposit to start the work.

He was happy to have found his first opportunity to work in Port-au-Prince. He put his best foot forward and built the family the best closet they had ever seen. My father was proud to hand to his brother and sister some of the money he'd earned so they could buy groceries for their apartment. He felt proud of his financial contribution, and established himself as a helper and not a freeloader.

At first, Samuel was not too thrilled with my father's choice to come to Port-au-Prince in search of a job. He thought that his younger brother was going to be a burden for him to bear. Nevertheless, he supported his younger brother and helped him get hired at the Emballage Adventist packaging company.

When my father got hired at the packaging company, he did such a good job and showed such great enthusiasms to learn and to work, that he soon became a supervisor, a spokesperson, and a team leader. He was so well-loved and respected that one of the drivers, whose name was Apollon, made it known to his coworkers that Zachari was his favorite colleague.

As the designated driver of the company's truck, Apollon routinely requested that my father be part of his team. When they traveled to different major cities of Haiti to pack and move clients' furniture and other belongings, Apollon always reserved the front passenger seat for my dad.

I found it interesting that my father, with only a middle school education, could be so intelligent and so wise as to prosper wherever he went. He told me that as a team leader, he was the intermediary for the clients and his team members. He communicated with the clients, who, most of the time, were Francophones and Anglophones.

How did my father do it with only a middle school

education? Why have I not done the same with two master's degrees?

Zachari said that the clients always treated him with respect and compassion. He had such a great relationship and rapport with the clients that they used to not only give him great tips, but they also offered him their cars and furniture for a low price before they left Haiti. My father became the middleman between the workers under him, and the clients for whom he worked. He also connected some of the people in his community with the clients' sales. When the clients were selling their items at a discounted price and my father did not have the funds to purchase the items, he would put the word out to the community, and people who had the money took advantage of the opportunity.

He was a man of honor who cared about the people with whom he worked, and he took care of them as much as he could. In private, he publicly shared the lucrative tips that he received from the clients. He became a Joseph to his older coworkers who started to become envious of his popularity and influence. He knew of their hatred, but he still chose to treat them with respect, knowing that his lofty position was a ministry. He kept in mind his past, his humble beginning, and where he came from, so that he could use it to fuel his destiny and his future.

At the packaging company, my father was promoted. The promotion enabled him to go to some of the clients' homes. One day, he was sent to work at the house of an officer of the American Embassy. He did not know at the time that the man whose furniture he'd come to pack worked at the embassy. As he always did, he started a conversation in French with the man who happened to be white. While conversing casually, my father told the man that he would love to visit his country someday. It is important to note that my father had no knowledge of the man's country of origin, but he was certain the man's country must have been the promised land. He did not expect anything significant out of the conversation, he was simply being friendly while working for his client.

I wonder how my father used his middle school education to communicate with the client in French? How did he learn English to converse with Anglophone clients?

He was surprised to find out that his conversation with the client and his audacity to hope paved the way for me and my siblings to be in the United States today. When my father told the man that he wanted to visit his country, he asked my father in French, "Qu'est-ce qui t'enpêche?" which means "What is stopping you?"

He asked my father if he had a passport and if he was married, to which my father responded in the affirmative. My father had always had faith that he would visit the US at some point in his life. He'd acted on his faith and applied for a passport before he knew that he would have an opportunity to apply for a visa. The man told my father to take his passport to the embassy the next day. My father was a smart man; he knew what he wanted in life, and had positioned himself to get it. He was a believer in himself and in God. He was an opportunist, a go-getter, and a man who kept hope alive in his heart. I wanted to be like my father when I grew up.

On the next day after his conversation with the man, he went down to the embassy and the same client granted him a visa. Toussaint Louverture did not kill all the white men in Haiti during the revolution, because he believed that they were not all evil. I am forever grateful to the white man who gave my father the visa out of the goodness of his heart. What he did for my father did not only bless him, it blessed me, and it will bless my children's children.

My father is still alive as I write this paragraph. At 69 years of age, he still works as if he was 21 years old. Hope is still alive in his heart. Although he is an accomplished man who is living his dream, he has done well in his life because he embraced what he had, and he worked hard at improving it every chance he had.

Samuel, who had asked my father to go back to Cap-Haïtien, the second major city in Haiti, also did well in Port-au-Prince, but my father got on an airplane before his brother did and came to the United States to become a US citizen. In fact, when his brother got to the US a few years later, he had difficulties getting his immigration papers in order. He was in New York and had received a deportation letter, but the same little brother that he'd ordered to go back home because he did not have enough money to support him back in Port-au-Prince a decade, invited him to come to Florida so that he could take care of him financially and help him get his papers in order.

My father met the needs of his older brother when he needed it the most. He embraced his life, and he worked hard to change his condition of living so that he could meet the needs of his younger siblings, and of those in his community. Because my father could visualize himself on an airplane despite his lack of education and financial resources, less than two decades later, he was constantly flying back-and-forth between Miami and Port-au-Prince. To God be the glory!

If my father could find success in his life despite his childhood, what is stopping you? If he survived being raised by his siblings and walking to and from school for two hours each way, what is hindering you? Embrace your life and position yourself to take advantage of any opportunity that life gives you, and never give up despite the obstacles that you may face.

I believe that you can be successful, and you will be successful if you embrace your life and work hard at changing your situation for the better. Don't allow fear to stop you from moving forward. Are you ready to succeed using your own childhood? If your childhood was worse than my father's, I want to encourage you to keep on reading; you will be inspired to do something with your childhood story. Someone will greatly benefit from your story and your experiences up to this point in your life.

My father
I am so proud of you, Dad.

Chapter 3
My Mother's Childhood in Haiti

I will now share with you my mother's childhood stories and how she embraced her life to become who she is today. Her childhood was different than that of my father's in many respects, but I believe that it will edify and motivate you as well.

Marie Suzette was the name given to her when she was born February of 1950. She was born in a communal section of Acul du Nord. My mother told my siblings and me how challenging her childhood was, and what a miracle it was for her to have survived. She told us that her mother, Henriette, had given birth to three children before her, but they'd all died of unnatural causes. The rumor she heard as a child was that her three older siblings were murdered in the womb by powerful enchanters. Apparently, her mother had many enemies in the neighborhood where she was born. It was believed that my mother, too, was supposed to have died as a child, but the midwife who helped to deliver her as a baby was more powerful than the enchanters, because she was a God-fearing Baptist woman. My mother escaped death as an infant and was given a chance to live.

When she was three months old, she started swelling like a puffer fish ready to explode. One of her aunts, whose nickname was Zabo, and with whom she was temporarily living so that she could go to school for sewing and tailoring lessons, was present and rushed her to the nearby hospital. My mother's life was spared again.

Her childhood was not all that fun. She was never raped, molested, or physically abused by anyone, but her childhood was challenging. My mother told me that in the village where she lived, there was once a devastating flood that destroyed almost every home in its path. Many little children and adults died on that day.

My mother completed her middle school years while living with my aunt. She was a bright student who received the highest certificate of achievement in her school district for the middle school national exam. She said that it was such a big deal, that her small village talked about her achievements for weeks. The publicity attracted the attention of envious parents whose children did not do as well. Unfortunately, her father Maurice, who was a farmer, did not pay for her to continue with her education and move on to high school, which was not tuition-free in Haiti.

In those days, many Haitian parents who lived in the country side of Haiti called Acul du Nord did not believe in paying for their daughters to have a high school education. They believed in putting children to work, or at best, forcing them to learn a trade such as sewing for girls, and welding for boys. My mother shared with us that she still regrets the fact that her father refused to pay for her education. With her hunger for knowledge and her discipline to study, she could have been a physician, teacher, lawyer, or anything that she wanted to pursue. She embraced her lack of opportunities in life and took advantage of what she could obtain.

She grew up in a house with several siblings. Wilfride was the youngest son, Rose was the youngest daughter, and Lioto and Sylvestre were older than my mother. My mother's siblings did not have a good education either.

There remain many more children like my mother and her siblings, who are growing up in Haiti without an opportunity to improve their condition of living through formal education. Life is a living hell for children who are not allowed to learn due to a lack of opportunities.

On the infamous day of the heavy rain that resulted in a devastating flood, my mother's mother had just brought her food and some other items from home. She took some of the provisions that her mother had brought her and shared it with one of her aunts named Marie Joe.

My mother was about 19 years of age at the time. Her aunt was in the house trying to take care of the rapid rising water from the rain, while my mother held her aunt's three-year-old daughter. Unfortunately, her aunt drowned in her attempt to save the toddler and my mother.

My mother was left with the terrified toddler to find a way to escape death in the continuous surge of the water trapped in the house. She said that she saw a man who stepped on a piece of plywood and escaped to safety. When she attempted the same methodology, holding the toddler, she sank into a fast flowing six-feet body of water, which brutally and viciously separated her from the three-year-old. Unfortunately, the toddler and the mother died on that day.

What a horrible couple of hours to have experienced as a teenager. She saw so much death on that day that she was traumatized for years. She'd left her mother's house in search of knowledge and a trade, but she almost lost her own life.

My mother explained that the water carried her from the house, with other debris collected in the neighborhood. She was helpless, scared, and hopeless. As she was being tossed to and from, she noticed that there were different currents of water crashing into each other at a fast approaching intersection. Miraculously, one of the currents thrusted her violently at the doorstep of one of her cousins. She could have been electrocuted, for everyone knows that water is a conductor of electricity. As far as she knew, she was going to die on that day without seeing her parents one last time.

It must have been scary for anyone to see nothing but devastation all around as a child. Seeing that there was no way out, and that there would be no one to rescue her, must have been horrifying for my mother. What a horrible event in her childhood!

I imagined her to be traumatized by that experience. I was convinced that she had lost a part of her soul on that day. However, she explained that she was blessed that her life was spared, and that somehow the waters had carried her body to the door steps of her family. Although she wept bitterly for the many lives, especially the life of the toddler, that were lost in the flood, and she was saddened to see her aunt's house ravaged and destroyed forever, she was grateful to be alive and to have, once again, seen her parents and her family members who had escaped a horrible death by drowning.

As a child, she embraced her life because children are, most of the time, more willing to accept and adapt to life's situations and make the best out of them. When my mother told us the story about the loss of her aunt and baby cousin, she was no longer sad, because she understood that her past made her who she is today. She often refers to that event in her childhood to say that the Lord was with her, and that He had a special purpose for her life. You may ask today what was the reason that caused the Lord to spare Marie Suzette's life from the flood and the evil enchanters. I can tell you that the Lord protected my mother's life, and that He watched over her childhood, allowing many circumstances to shape her world view. God used my mother's childhood situations to prepare her for the noble career of raising children who would have a positive influence on the people around them.

Had the Lord not spared my mother's life, you would not be reading this book right now. Because my mother survived her childhood, my younger sister, Rodeline, is a nurse practitioner in Virginia. She is providing medical care for those in need. Rodeline was inspired to become a nurse and care for the sick because of our mother's childhood.

Seeing my mother sick all the time was so painful to my little sister that she vowed to take care of the sick and alleviate as much pain as possible from the world. Therefore, Rodeline's childhood propelled her to a nursing career. My youngest sister, Frandeline, is an accountant and a counselor. She has a heart for people, and would do everything in her power to help those in need.

My mother's childhood experiences prepared her to

minister to those in need, to listen to the problems of others, and offer sound advice. My sisters are both mothers of great children for whom they strive daily to provide for. Elora, Sarina, Elijah, and Lilly have a better childhood than their grandmother Suzette, because she embraced the life she was given, and made it better for the next generation.

There is always a purpose to our suffering. That is why we must all embrace our life. We must never forget or dismiss our childhood events. Something or someone great and powerful will come out of our childhood pain and suffering.

My mother told us of another time when, as a child, she was so sick that her skin was literally melting off her body. No one knew what was happening to her body due to the scarcity of medical care in her remote village. She explained that, somehow, she was healed. It is still unknown what went wrong with her.

It is amazing to hear my precious mother narrate her childhood events. She always spoke as if the Lord was in control of every event in her childhood. She spoke of the times when she would walk many miles just to attend school, carrying the only book that she knew the teacher was going to use on that day. She always looked forward to going back to school, but unfortunately, it did not happen for her as a child. Her parents did not make it a priority to pay for her education.

On July 2017, I received an email from a parent who shared with me that her daughter, who was probably nine or ten years old, wanted to take French lessons. The little girl was smart, and she studied the language on her own. Imagine her mother not being able to afford French lessons for her. Imagine how devastated and saddened that little girl would be. Imagine the humiliation of the mother and father who wanted to help, but financially could not. Sadly, it must have been how my mother felt as a child when her parents could no longer afford to send her to school. What a crime against a young mind to not be given the rights to a great education.

My siblings and I had a rough childhood with our mother's constant sickness, but we were blessed that she was alive to nurture us as much as her health allowed. She lost her mother at the age of 22. In Haiti, being 22 is equivalent to being 15 in the United States of America. That means my mother lost her mother when she needed her the most.

Her father was still alive when her mother passed away, but he died 20 years later at the age of 85. She was still trying to figure life out when she lost her dear mother. She embraced her life and clung to her remaining aunts and many good Samaritans at the Seventh-day Adventist church—where she was a member—who were willing to help her understand life.

My mother embraced her life and left her father's house to find a job to provide for her younger brother, Wilfrid, and her younger sister, Rose. She moved from Cap-Haïtien to Port-au-Prince, which is the capital of Haiti, because her chances of getting employment in Haiti were greater in Port-au-Prince than in Cap-Haïtien.

After her mother passed, she was concerned about not only her life, but that of her youngest siblings. She assumed the role of the mother and went out into the cold and lonely world to find her daily bread. One of her mother's good friends named Yaya took her to Port-au-Prince, where she stayed with her best friend, Anocia. Yaya's daughter also lived there. While staying with Yaya for a while, my mother went out daily to search for a job, but she was not able to find employment as she'd hoped.

Life was hard for her as a young woman who did not have a job, and who was living with a friend. My mother told me that her good friend, who was such an angel to her, brought her food every day from her job. She confessed that it was embarrassing to not be able to provide for herself a meal and a place to stay. She was tormented when she found out that one of the people living at her friend's house thought that she was taking advantage of Anocia. She was emotionally hurt, frustrated and confused, because she had done everything in her power to find a job, but was unsuccessful. Although it was a blessing for her friend to provide for her temporarily, my mother knew that she had to find another way. After all, she was poor, but she was a woman of dignity whose sole purpose of coming to Port-au-Prince was to find employment to provide for the younger siblings who were left behind.

My mother decided that she would move out of her best friend's home and move in with her godfather, Rigaud. I grew up hearing her talk about how much of a blessing Rigaud was. She found shelter and food at his house, and she felt less judged there. After a while, she began to struggle with the idea of living with her godfather's family. She was getting older; around the age of 24 or 25 by then.

One day, Riguad's wife said to her, "I saw your father at the market place, but he did not give me any money to help with you."

My mother was, once again, devastated and decided that she would move out. She was blessed with a job based on the sewing lessons that she took after graduating from middle school. Her duties were to sew several different color sequins on cloths and make them speckled. With her earnings, she rented a small apartment and moved in with a female roommate. Soon after, she married my father, whom she had met through my uncle Samuel at a Seventh-day Adventist church in Carrefour, Diquini. My father proposed to her a few months after they'd initially met. I forgot to mention an interesting part of her teenage years relative to her first boyfriend.

Prior to moving in with Anocia, my mother had a little boyfriend back in her village. In the late 1960s there were no cellular phones, internet, or social media. Living in cities that were miles apart, they had no way of keeping in touch. Unfortunately, or fortunately, she lost all contact with him and met my father. It was only a few years later, after she accepted the proposal to marry my father, that her ex-boyfriend found her in Port-au-Prince. I can only imagine what her life would have been had she not married my father.

In all honesty, I secretly think that her true love was her first boyfriend, but I could be wrong. Nevertheless, my mother was a woman of her word. She had already agreed to marry my father, and embraced her life and remained with him.

Should she have followed her heart? I think that embracing her life and honoring her wedding vows was one of the best decisions she has ever made.

Despite her childhood circumstances, my mother is a happy grandmother with six grandchildren. She has learned how to write and speak English. She has worked in the United States for several years and earned a living. Now she can read books in both French and English, and is able to learn about any topic of her interests. She owns a MacBook and is always online researching various websites through Google. While that may not have any significant meaning to you, there are many people in the Haitian community where she grew up who may still not be able to turn on a computer, let alone browse the internet. In fact, there might be people in America in 2017 who still do not have an email address.

My mother learned how to drive, and was recently working on her GED. At the age of 68, she has an email address and a Facebook page. I am so proud of my mother's achievements and her efforts to learn what children today take for granted.

She was always sick in Haiti, especially after she met my father. She was under the influence of witchcraft, but she was never diagnosed with any cancer or any known disease in conventional western medicine. Now living in the United States, she is enjoying perfect health. She has had several medical check-ups and learned that her health is perfect. Considering her age, she is not on any medication.

She embraced her lack of education and happily raised her children. She enjoys spending time with her grandchildren.

Having worked hard, through sickness and lack of financial resources, devoid of the love and presence of a man who was working in the United States to provide for us back in Haiti, today she reaps the benefits of seeing her own children receive the education that she was not allowed to acquire, and live the life that she could not afford to live as a young adult.

She could have been bitter about her childhood, she could have even competed with us, her children, to keep us at her level of education. Instead, my lovely and beautiful mother did everything in her power to give us a good life. She positioned us to take advantage of any opportunity that life might present to us. My siblings and I had a rough childhood with our mother's constant sickness, but we were blessed that she was alive to nurture us as much as her health allowed it.

My mother's struggles as a teenager paved the way for my little sisters. They never had to go on a desperate search for a job because their rent depended on it. They worked because they wanted to make their own money. My mother was alive and did her best to provide a loving home for them. They could continue with their education because Mother was there to make it happen. My sisters were never homeless, they never worried about their future like mother did when she had no place to live, and they never had to stay with a friend who provided a meal for them. Their experiences as a child were nowhere close to half of what Mother experienced, because she did an excellent job sheltering them.

I shared my mother's childhood story to help inspire you, and hopefully encourage you to embrace your own childhood. I want you to embrace your own life no matter what hellish situation you may be facing as you read this book.

I am sure that twenty to forty years from now, you will reap the fruits of your hard labor. The fruits can come through your children, your accomplishments in the world, or the lives of others you have touched.

Embrace your life as a parent, and do your best to keep your children from experiencing the same pain that you experienced. Be grateful for every day that you have with them, for tomorrow is not promised.

One of my greatest fears as a parent is to die without leaving enough financial support for my children to survive. My grandmother died when my mother was very young, and consequently, her life was miserable. Imagine how much harder her life would have been if her mother had passed away when she was still a toddler. That is why I pray that you embrace your life as a parent, and cherish every moment that you have with your children. There is no guarantee that you will enjoy another day with them. They will miss you greatly, but the pain of not having a place to stay, the undignified moments of being hungry and not having food to eat, and the horror of not being able to acquire the basic things in life will be harder to handle.

The world is filled with orphans who wished that their parents were still alive. I have three cousins who lost their parents when they reached their teenage years. Their father, Lioto, was one of my mother's brothers. Lioto died, leaving his wife with three beautiful children to raise. She became sick and died a few years later, leaving her children at the mercy of a cruel and indifferent world.

I praise God for a Baptist church in Port-au-Prince who cared for my cousins as much as they could. It still pains me to think about my cousins, because they are still in Haiti struggling for their daily bread.

They spent a month living in our house when their mother was alive. We played together as children, and were sad when they left. I try not to think about them living as orphans, and I promised that I would take care of them once I started making some money. If my father and mother made it, if they found a way to live out their dream despite their childhood, so can I.

I believe that I will have enough money to take care of the orphans in my family and in the world. That is my dream, and I will live it out one day.

Our children are not exempt from becoming orphans, therefore, we must work diligently to prepare them to live alone in this world of indifference. I sincerely pray that the Lord will give us long life and good health, that way we can be in our children's lives to provide for them for as long as they need our help. I pray that God shows us how to individually embrace our life, so that we can give our children our best years. Let us prepare our children to embrace their own life. Let us teach them that their life has a purpose, and that they were born to meet a need. Someone in their generation will be blessed by their knowledge, someone's life will be spared by their research, and somebody's child will develop a love of learning because of their teaching philosophy. Let us prepare our children to survive if we were to perish tomorrow.

We must embrace our life knowing that tomorrow is not promised to anyone of us. We might wake up today, and our life is taken away from us in the next hour in a million different ways. Natural disasters can strike at any time, as well as random acts of terror (both domestic and foreign). The discovery of a tumor in our body can surprise us.

Our survival is constantly threatened by life's uncertainties; therefore, we must embrace the present, for we do not possess the future. We must do our best today, as if tomorrow was not an option. We may not be able to do too much to protect our little ones; there are certain situations that are out of our hands. But let us vow to use our best human efforts to provide for and protect the precious children that the Lord has entrusted unto us.

I read in the news that in Jacksonville, Florida, two white nurses were removed from duty at a naval hospital for unethical actions. They had uploaded a video to their social media pages of two black newborn babies whose bodies they manipulated to make them dance to rap music. One of the most disheartening things in the video was that one of the evil nurses gave the middle finger and said, "This is how I currently feel about my mini Satans." She was referring to the newborn black babies.

I use this story to say that your children are growing up in a world filled of hateful people, deranged individuals, and hypocrites who smile in public and frown in private. Most of them are individuals who do not embrace their life, and choose to serve a purpose that meets the needs of their community. The nurses' job was to provide medical care, but the need they should have met was to care for those baby humans, and not take advantage of them and call them "mini Satans." Who knows what else they did to other non-white children?

I wish that I could change this world and make it a better place for everyone to coexist in love and harmony. I will make the world a better place one person at a time, and I will do so by meeting one need at a time. I encourage you to do the same.

My lovely mother
I will always love you, Mom!

Her lovely six grand-children

Chapter 4
My Interesting Childhood in Haiti

I will now share my childhood story to help you see how my parents' resilience affected my life. My childhood was a direct result of my parents' combined experiences. I pray that you learn something helpful as you read about my childhood.

I grew up in Haiti in the late 1900s, where the education system was as poor as the citizens of the country itself. What I mean by "poor" is that the country did not have the resources that most developed countries must possess to help students learn in school. The reason Haiti did not have the resources needed to educate its children is well-known to the rest of the world. Haiti was and still is paying for the awesome and irrefutable victory over the French white supremacist army and government who sought to enslave the people they stole, exploited, and violated from West Africa in perpetuity.

After the Haitians' Godly and legendary victory over the French devils, Haitian men and women had to struggle against the deceptive politics of other racist governments who kept destabilizing the country. They killed our pigs, they destroyed our economy, and they stole our wealth. Consequently, many Haitian children like myself suffered and continue to suffer greatly.

I struggled in primary school, elementary school, and high school. Back then, students used to be severely punished at school, with a stick or a ruler, for not memorizing history, multiplication table, and other academic materials that students should understand and not memorize. I did not really have anyone to help me at home. My dad started to help me in kindergarten, but he was blessed with a visa to go to the United States of America to work and make life for us in Haiti a little better financially.

I remember before my father left Haiti, we were a happy family. He used to play soccer with me and teach me how to shoot the ball. He bought me several soccer balls and several tennis shoes to play the game. My siblings and I used to look forward to his return from work every evening. He used to religiously bring us sweet treats from work, and occasionally he used to take us to the park. He took us to get ice cream, and he took us to the beach on Sundays. He took time to teach us how to swim, but I was terrified by the depth of the water.

I remember how much of a strong and dedicated worker he was. He worked hard to renovate our first house. He put a lot of time and energy in expanding and beautifying it. My father was my hero. He and his older brother were great carpenters; together they made our dining and living room furniture.

One day, my father was repainting our house and he turned to me and said, "Soon you will be old enough to repaint this house." Although it did not happen, because we moved out of the house eight to ten years after my father left Haiti, I understand that the true meaning of his words was more meaningful than repainting the house.

Going to church on the weekend with my family was also fun. My father used to buy us the best little suits, ties, and shoes. Raised as Seventh-day Adventist, on the weekends we did not work. We spent our Fridays and Saturdays at the church among friends and family. My mother used to prepare a feast for us to eat and share with our weekend guests. My father was a deacon at our church, and he was also part of a men's choir. We, the children, had no issues sleeping at night. We feared no evil, because our father was home with us, and our mother provided a loving home for us.

Father used to take us to school. We did not have a car, so we used to catch the city bus. My mother picked us up from school, because my father did not get off work until later in the evening.

I cannot begin to express how beautiful my life was as a child before my dad left to go the United States to become a permanent legal resident. My dad loved us so much that he sent us to one of the best private schools in Port-au-Prince. He was not earning much money, but he did his best with what he had.

When I was a little boy, I did not know that nothing "good" lasts forever. I think that I have even heard or read somewhere that all good things must come to an end at some point. For me, it was the day my dad announced to us that he was moving to the United States of America on a five-year visa.

He took us to a party that his employers were having for him at his place of work. As a child, I enjoyed the party because there was plenty of food, music, and a recognition ceremony where my father received a certificate of achievement. I was proud of my dad's accomplishments, and loved the way his coworkers congratulated him. Although everyone had a great time at the party, my mother seemed a little distracted and aloof. Now that I am older and I am also married, I can empathize with my mother's true feelings of abandonment, and fear of having a dysfunctional family.

Imagine that you are left with three children to raise, protect, and feed. You must play both the father's and the mother's role. At that point, embracing your life as a single parent is the only thing that makes sense. My mother was probably in her early thirties when my father left, which means she was scared to death.

A week before my father's departure, several members of our church, close friends, neighbors, and family members came together to have a little going away party. It became a real fact to my siblings and mother that my dad was really leaving. We all wept like babies. That party was not fun at all. I'd known that my father was leaving very soon, but I had no idea how much different and hard life was going to be for us. We were going to move from heaven to hell.

When my father started packing his luggage, we congregated around him, attempting to soak up as much of his essence, as if to last us four to five years. Then, the most dreaded day arrived. One of my father's friends came to give us a ride to the, now, Toussaint Louverture International Airport in Port-au-Prince. It was one of the longest rides we had ever taken to the airport.

Everyone was sad and wished that it was a nightmare from which it was possible to wake up. I can only imagine what my dad's thoughts were at that time. He was still a young man; younger than I am right now as I write this book. He must have felt extreme pain and confusion as far as leaving us in Haiti alone, or going to the United States to provide. He embraced his life and accepted his dilemma. He had made his decision to invest in our future for the long run, and sacrifice our temporary utopic family bliss.

When we arrived at the airport, my father took his luggage and turned to give me one last hug. I did not want to let him go, but I knew that I could not hold him forever. He then turned and kissed and hugged my sisters. I am sure they were more hurt than I was, because they were younger. My dad finally embraced my mother one last time, and then he sadly walked away from us.

Embracing his new life, he headed toward security to show his boarding pass, and then entered the waiting area. We waited a while, hoping to see our dad one last time as he walked toward the plane. He was going to board a plane as he had predicted with his older brother back in Grand Rivière when he was 11 years old.

The airport in Port-au-Prince had a huge balcony where people could watch their loved ones as they left the terminal on foot to board the plane. We finally saw my dad walking out of the airport toward the runway. We were grateful that we had another opportunity to see our father. We waved at him, but we were not sure that he could see us. We cried again and continued to wave until he set his feet on the plane. We were then robbed of his presence.

We waited on the balcony to see the plane take off, and waved goodbye to our dad one last time. I was secretly hoping that my father was going to get off the plane and return home with us. It never happened. Instead, the plane took off and disappeared on the horizon while we gazed at the clouds and the empty, hollow sky.

On that day, I learned to embrace my life, and my mother learned to embrace her life as a single parent. Embracing our new life did not keep us from crying on the way to the airport, crying at the airport, and crying on the way back home from the airport. You can imagine how long the first night was at home without my father. Although slavery in Haiti ended in the early 1800s, I have partially experienced the deep sadness the slave children endured when the cruel and beast-like slave masters sold both parents to different plantations. At least I had hope to see my father one more time, but those slave children had no hope.

We did not have a telephone at home and could not communicate with our dad through email. We did not know if he'd made it to the US safely, or if anything terrible had happened. The only hope we had was to drive to downtown Port-au-Prince and pay a company called Teleco to have a few minutes to talk to my dad. I wish that we'd had access to all the new technology available today.

I have not been to Haiti in 20 years, but I have heard that almost everyone has a cell phone, if not a smart phone. They have access to Skype, WhatsApp, Imo, and plenty more apps that could have made communicating with my dad a little easier in the 1980s.

I am convinced that the flight to the United States of America was long and painful for my dad, even though it was the fulfillment of his dream. I imagined him reflecting on Haiti's political instability, and I thought that it must have been paralyzing.

The first couple of weeks living without my dad at home

was painful, but just as every other child in the world, my siblings and I quickly learned to adapt and embrace the life we now had without our dad's physical presence in the home.

In the 80s, most Haitian families used a cassette player to record a message to their family in the diaspora. Consequently, my mother bought some cassettes and we recorded our voices, telling our dad how much we missed him. We sang for him on the cassettes, and told him that we could not wait to see him again.

As children, we felt fulfilled that we had recorded our voices for our dad. We waited patiently for him to send us something back. We used to wonder how he reacted when listening to our little voices crying and singing through the cassettes. In the meanwhile, we accepted our fate and we thanked God every time we heard his voice, every time we received a package from him with toys, and every time he sent us money so that we could have food to eat. We embraced our new life knowing that our father loved us and that he was working hard for us overseas.

Our mother did an excellent job raising us alone. She was always positive about Dad. She kept us hoping that we would one day all be under the same roof living as a family again. She helped us live in the future, elevating our mind to a distant time when Dad would come back and take us to go live with him in the US.

We did not have a refrigerator at home, we did not have a microwave, but we had a small television set, which we used to drown our pain. We did not have an alarm system or guard dogs to keep us safe at night. Our mother kept us hopeful that her God would protect us against evil. We were not too unhappy that we lacked a few necessities, we simply missed our dad. We would have given up everything just to be with him.

Life went on, we grew a little older, we suffered a little here and there, but we embraced every moment of it. There were days when we cried, and there were days when we laughed and played. Our cornerstone mother kept us alive and hopeful.

One day, I felt a strong urge to pray for my father. I missed him greatly and thought that I would pray for his safety. I went to my room, which was also my sisters' room. We shared the same room, because I refused to sleep in a room alone for fear of being taken by Loup-Garou in the middle of the night. I fervently prayed that the Lord would shield my father and keep us healthy until we could meet again. That same week, my mother received news that my father was almost killed on I-95 in Miami, Florida.

Apparently, my father's car overheated and it caught on fire while driving. It was believed that my dad could not get out of the vehicle and was almost engulfed in flames. He was rescued by a passerby who gave him a helping hand. His life was spared and he came out of the burning vehicle safe and sound without a scratch. We were very happy to hear that Dad was alive and safe. In my childish faith and being grateful to the Lord, I went back to my room and offered a prayer of thanksgiving to the Lord who preserved my father's life.

On another occasion, my father was returning to his home from work. At the time, he worked in Miami and he did not have a car. He was at the bus stop waiting for the bus late at night. A thief came and pulled a gun on him and ordered him to lay flat on the ground. The man asked my dad for his wallet and his watch, but he did not hurt him. I am happy that my father survived the robbery and was not killed or physically harmed. Every time we heard bad news, it motivated us to pray more zealously for Dad

There was another occasion when my father almost died. He was sick, throwing up while driving from work. He threw up so much that he pulled off the road and went to a gas station on Biscayne Boulevard in Miami to regain his strength. He leaned against the steering wheel as he rested and supported his weakening body. Unfortunately, he fainted and lost consciousness for an entire day. He regained his consciousness after 24 hours, and learned that his good friend, Veronique, had seen his parked vehicle at the gas station. She called 911 and saved his life. I am forever grateful to Veronique, who was the angel who saved my father's life.

Without her good Samaritan heart, my father would have died. I would have stayed in Haiti without an opportunity to minister to you. Part of embracing our life meant to keep our dad in prayer so that the Lord could protect him and prosper him. He would have died in Miami if the Lord had not spared his life.

Prior to my father's departure from Haiti, my mother's quality of life was decent. I cannot recall her being constantly in pain and sad. I remember her as being beautiful, vibrant, strong, creative, and a chef. As far as I knew, her relationship with my father was great, but I learned that even though there was no verbal or physical abuse, my parents' relationship was not that great.

I do not remember seeing my mother suffer from any kind of illness prior to my father's departure to the US. It was only after my dad left and we were on our own that I began to see another side of my mother. She became acquainted with grief and pain.

She told us that after our father left, she had a dream on the same night. She said that she saw herself walking somewhere not too far from where my father used to work and where I used to attend school. She said that she saw darkness all around her. Suddenly, and without any warning, she was surrounded by a deep ocean. She said that it was so scary and felt so real that she prayed in the dream and asked the Lord, "Kote map fè la?" in Haitian Creole. Essentially, she asked the Lord how will she get out of the threating body of water that engulfed her.

Having prayed and asked for direction, she looked to her left and saw a little pathway within the water that led her out of the water. She woke up knowing that life was going be tough, but somehow the Lord would make a way out of it all.

She understood that it was a clear revelation of her future and what was to take place in her life.

The Creator was forewarning her and informing her that she was going to have a hard time, and that it was going to happen suddenly. The good news is that within the dream was the key to Mother's deliverance from the evil that was to befall her. She was going to find herself in complete psychological darkness, and her body was going to be submitted and subjugated to much pain. But prayer would cause God to make a way out for her. The promise of the pathway in the dream kept my mother hopeful that the waters of impending difficulties were not going to drown her.

As revealed in her dream, my poor mother was always gravely ill, confused, and depressed. There were rumors that were circulating at the time. Some of the neighbors claimed that our family members envied Mother for the house in which my dad had left her, and for the possibility of our family traveling to the US. We were told that someone sold my mother's soul to the devil, and one of my aunts allegedly promised her that they were going to carry her out of the house wrapped in a body bag.

I remember my mother telling us that one of our aunts asked to borrow her personal head wrap, claiming that she did not have a clean head wrap of her own. My mother told us that she did not make a big deal out of lending her own "mouchwa" head wrap to my aunt, because she was one of her in-laws.

Unfortunately, in witchcraft, evil men and women can use anything that has an individuals' sweat, hair, and DNA to conjure up a spell against them. Hence, my mother's head wrap was used against her to bring her sudden unbearable headaches and other woes.

My mother suffered from all kinds of ailments, disorders, and maladies, for which conventional medicines had no cure. She had chronic stomach aches, chronic headaches, violent seizures, chronic pain in her left arm and in her right leg, and at one point, she was demon possessed.

One lovely Sunday, my mother was in the kitchen preparing one of the best meals ever. She was cooking a traditional Haitian meal. The meal consisted of rice, red beans, and a fine and delicious chicken. It was a meal that we were looking forward to eating, as were other Haitian children all over Haiti. It is a custom for most families in Haiti to have a feast on Sundays. It is a great tradition that Haitian children enjoy. They may not eat too well during the week, but they could always look forward to Sunday's dinner.

While mother was in the kitchen getting ready to prepare the food, she had a young woman—who practically raised me as a child—helping her in the kitchen. The young woman's name was Simone. Simone was an angel in the sense that through the years when my mother was unable to truly take care of us due to her constant sickness, Simone became our second mother, even if she was still a young woman.

We were not fortunate enough to have an electric stove, nor did we have a crock pot. The way we cooked our food was by means of a Haitian style stove with charcoal burning, and pots sitting directly on them. They are like the grills used in the US on July 4th, when Americans barbecue their meat. My mother and Simone were cooking when suddenly, just as my mother had seen in her dream, she collapsed and was heading straight for the hot grills. My mother was experiencing a terrible seizure in the kitchen, which was filled with hot coals and burning pots. If Simone had not been in the kitchen to catch and redirect my mother's body toward a safer fall, she would have possibly suffered third-degree burns. She would have been burnt and disfigured forever.

My mother's seizure in the kitchen turned into four-days of unconscious, scary gesticulations, and a full-fledged demonic possession. Our anticipated Haitian feast was ruined and disrupted, for our mother was so out of it that she did not recognize us for four days. The neighbors gathered up. It was a scary scene. They came with their Bibles and hymnals, and they prayed their hearts out, asking the Lord to deliver my mother and to restore her soul.

I am so thankful for great neighbors such as Madame Mathurin, who rushed in to help. My siblings and I were devastated and scared. We were no longer hungry. We prayed, cried, and begged the Lord to help our mother regain her consciousness, and to recognize us as her children.

That Sunday night, my mother was so sick that I slept at madam Mathurin's house, because I was afraid of my own mother. She was not herself, and therefore I was afraid that the demon(s) who took over her soul and body would hurt me. Thank God that through prayer and a lot of natural Haitian remedies made with leaves, salt, and burning pepper, my mother's soul returned to her.

Oh, how I'd wished that my father had never left. That was the last time that I saw my mother possessed. But unfortunately, she continued to be sick and to suffer from different types of nuisances. She was plagued with nightmares, she was depressed, mentally and physically tired, and she still had to find ways to feed her children. She used to hear voices calling her name in the middle of the night and throughout the day. The voices that she was hearing were the familiar voices of family members, friends, and even her foes.

There is a well-known superstition in Haiti that says, "If you hear voices calling you and you answer, you will die." Well, my mother has never told us whether she ever responded to those voices, but one thing that I know for sure is that my mother was experiencing schizophrenic spells.

I know that there is a God, or else how do you explain a woman under schizophrenic spells raising three children without any conventional medicine for schizophrenia? Through prayer and Haitian natural remedies alone, my mother found the strength to live and raise her children. I believe that her faith and optimism kept her alive. She had faith that the same God who revealed to her in a dream the way her life was going to unfold after the departure of her husband, would eventually make a way out of all her sickness and all the suffering that she was experiencing.

God did not give her a timeframe, and He did not reveal to her exactly what she was going to endure. God simply showed her the beginning and the end of her misery. Therefore, she embraced her suffering knowing that one day the Lord would deliver her. She knew that it was only a matter of time, and for that reason, she kept a positive attitude for as long as she could.

I remember my mother used to always tell me that the seizures she was having would eventually stop, and at that time she would be whole again. Now that I am older, I find it fascinating that a woman who had constant seizures for several years could suddenly be healed and never have another episode for over 20 plus years. That is encouraging to me, and I hope that it encourages you to embrace your current health situations knowing that the same God who did it for my mother can do it for you as well. The great news is that my loving mother would someday be well, but until then, she continued to suffer unimaginably.

One day, in broad daylight, she was sleeping in one of the bedrooms that led to our backyard. It was the early 80s. I do not remember how old I was, but I must have been younger than ten years old. My siblings and I were playing outside as children do. The back door leading to the bedroom was securely locked, and there was no access in except through the front door. I went inside of the house to get some water because I was thirsty from running around with the other kids. I found my mother still asleep, but covered in blood. I screamed to wake my mother up and asked her what was wrong and why she was bleeding so much. She woke up confused and asked me in Haitian Creole, "ki sa'm gen yen (what's wrong with me)?"

She asked me to get her a mirror so that she could look at her face. She was surprised to see that she was cut, and to learn that she had been stabbed right above her left eye. It was one of the scariest moments of my life. I called my little sisters, along with the neighbors, and we were all surprised to find out that whoever stabbed my mother was also trying to take the blood out of the house through the back door. Lord knows for what purpose!

We saw a blood trail that led all the way to the outside latrine. We knew that it had to be the Lord who kept my mother from losing her eyes, and ultimately her life. She could have bled to death, or they could have stabbed her in the heart, but praise be to the Maker, Creator, and Protector of life! The enemy was not allowed to take my mother's life.

When I reflect on what happened on that gloomy day, I feel extremely grateful that my siblings and I were not in the house when the intruder came with his or her nefarious intentions and mission to draw innocent blood. Praise God that we were outside playing, and that we were spared such a horrific sight. Imagine the psychological battles that were raging in my mind; the hate I felt for the people I thought were responsible for my mother's misery. My life was a living hell growing up, but there was a purpose to all of it.

There were days when I had nothing to eat. My father would send money to support us, but by the time it reached my mother's sick hands and troubled mind, the money was spent repaying lenders and paying our school tuition. As a little boy, I was always afraid. I had developed anxiety attacks. I hated nights because I was also plagued with nightmares. I did not want to sleep in the same bed with my mother, because I was afraid that she would have a seizure and that I would be hurt. I was sad that my father was not there to protect us against those who wanted to hurt us.

My father did not abandon us; he was simply away working multiple jobs to provide for us. I loved him so dearly, because he did his best to provide a better life for us in the long run. I used to lay awake in my bed terrified of what might happen to us or our mother, knowing that there was no man in our home to protect us or fight for us.

My uncle Wilfrid, my mother's younger brother, used to come and spend the night with us, and sometimes a few months at a time. I used to love it when he was around, because it made me feel safe. But he was not always there because he had his own life.

My uncle had no idea how safe I felt simply because he was around. There were times that at approximately three o'clock in the morning, the witching hour, I used to hear the strange and scary sounds of women's high heel dress shoes walking around incessantly in our house. My little heart used to pound faster than usual for hours, and kept me up half of the night. I felt as if I was going to have a heart attack. When I would finally fall asleep, I experienced constant sleep paralysis on a nightly basis. I was miserable, dreading night time and the fear of the enchanters who wanted us dead.

One day, I was so sick that my mother said I spent an entire night trying to kill myself in my sleep. She said that I kept trying to dive, head first, toward the concrete floor of our old bedroom. We did not own nice wood floors or cushy carpet. We had a rugged and rocky looking floor. My mother told me that she could not sleep the entire night watching me. I imagine she was probably praying for me, asking the Lord to spare my young life.

The next day when I woke up, I didn't remember a thing. I thought I'd slept all night. I did, though, feel my mind going in and out of consciousness. I was sick, scared, hungry, sad, and asking myself why life had to be this hard for us. I am thankful that my mother was not out of her mind the night that my soul was hijacked.

I missed my dad and wished he was home with us. I understood that he had to work for us, but his presence was worth more than money. I hated my situation and wanted a better life for myself and that of the members of my family.

Outside of me hearing the sound of women's high heel shoes clicking, both my siblings and I used to hear strange noises in and outside of our house. We were told that it was haunted. With all that going on in my house, I was still expected to perform well at school. Unfortunately, I had a hard time juggling the dark drama at home, and being humiliated at school for not understanding math and mastering grammar.

My childhood was a wreck. I used to pray day and night, asking the Lord to heal my mother and to change our living situation. Sometimes, I would be at school crying for my mother and crying about not having money to buy lunch. I was never raped or physically abused, but I grew up psychologically damaged because I could not understand the reason why my family members would, allegedly, inflict such atrocious pain on my dear mother, and indirectly on myself and my siblings.

I remember things got so bad that my mother had to take us out of school one afternoon. Someone claimed that my little sister, Frandeline, was almost poisoned. Some of our neighbors were hostile toward my mother, attempting to fight and kill her. I was living in constant fear for both my mother and my life. There were also criminals called "Zenglendo" in Haitian Creole, who would shoot their guns all night, vandalize homes, and hurt families. They were a feared group of individuals who were probably poor, destitute puppets used to destabilized the country by domestic and foreign powers. Thank God we were spared the criminal activities. No one broke into our house at night to hurt us, as I always feared would eventually happen.

I was constantly sad seeing my mother cry. It was unbearable seeing her sick, helpless, and lonely. I remember on one occasion she went to Cap-Haïtien. I was so scared that my mother was never coming back home—that her sickness would finally get the best of her—that I began to pray for her. To make matters worse, my mother sowed for my sisters two beautiful black and white dresses to attend her own funeral. She also made me a shirt, and I guess she must have said to herself, "If I do not survive, my children will at least have nice, brand-new clothes to wear to my funeral."

It dawned on me at that time that my mother had finally given up and surrendered her will to her spiritual oppressors. Up to that point, I had never seen my mother in such a state of despair. She was the same faithful woman who kept telling me that she was going to be healed soon, and who, since my father had left, started having regular family prayer before we went to bed. I learned and memorized Psalms 23, which is one of my favorite Bible verses. It says something analogous to the following sentence: even when I pass through a valley where the shadow of death encompasses me, I have no fear, simply because I know that the Lord is with me.

I memorized and recited Psalms 46, which encouraged me to know that the Lord is my refuge; He is my strength and my helper even in trouble. Psalms 121 is another one of my favorites. It helped me to elevate my mind and find the Lord who created the heavens and the earth. I found a spiritual anchoring place in Psalms 121, which says that the Lord who watches over my life, my future, my safety, never takes a nap, and that He does not sleep.

As a child, it was reassuring to know there was a being who made it its duty to protect the vulnerable and forgotten ones. We recited those psalms every night, and we sang songs from our Seventh-day Adventist hymnal that helped us feel safe. They were powerful because we believed in what we were singing and reciting. They ministered to our soul and calmed our fears.

One of my favorite nightly songs from the French hymnal had a powerful verse: "Seigneur je fais ma prière, sous ton aile je m'endors, Heureux de savoir qu'un père plein d'amour veille au dehors." Here is the English translation: Lord, this is my prayer. Under your wings I fall asleep happy to know that I have a loving father who is watching over me from the outside.

My mother was that same woman who played the role of priestess in our home. She was my spiritual hero, but now I saw her as defeated and conquered. She had never given up on her faith before, and she had never given up on the power of the "Gran mèt," the Haitian word for "God." I started weeping bitterly and asking the Lord to bring my mother back from the man-made hell from which she had desperately tried to escape.

I assumed the role of substitute priest and went after those demons in prayer. I felt my soul cry within me, begging the Creator to spare my mother. It was time for me to act on my faith and help my mother in the family spiritual warfare. My childhood was not worth living, I thought, if my mother died while in Cap-Haïtien. If the Lord did not answer my prayer and bring my mother back in one piece, I would stop believing in Him and would seek to avenge my mother's death. As a matter of fact, I said that I would kill myself if my mother did not survive the many attacks on her soul.

I started having bipolar thoughts. On one hand, I assumed the role of the family intercessor, and on the other hand, I felt like a victim who wanted revenge. I can tell you honestly that, as a child, I did not intellectually know that I was supposed to embrace my life no matter the circumstances. I had done it instinctively, but not intentionally. I did that when I assumed the role of the family priest, but I did not embrace my life when I thought of suicide and revenge.

I had no idea that the Lord was going to use everything I went through to make me the man that I am today. I did not know that my mother was going to survive and still be alive as I type these words in the parking lot of the Emmet O'Neal Library in Birmingham. I am glad that the Lord did not allow me to take my own life, and I am thankful that I did not have to seek revenge.

As I reflect on my mother's sad and scary past, I am more than grateful to the Lord, to all the neighbors, and to Simone. It is good to embrace life instinctively, just as children do, to help them cope with life, but it is important to make educated decisions in every aspect of life to embrace our life no matter what.

Who am I today? I am still a child living in a now 42-year-old adult body. I still call on the Lord when I am scared, and I still pray for my mother, who continues to treat me as her "little boy." I still recite my favorite psalms for protection, as well as some of my mother's favorite psalms. She loved to recite Psalms 3, which helped her to know that when she lays down and sleeps, she can be sure that the Lord will wake her up, because He sustains her.

She was encouraged by the verse that says not to be afraid of ten thousand enemies who seek to destroy her life. In Psalms 27, she found comfort in the words of David, particularly when he says that he considers the Lord as his light, his salvation, and his strength. Psalms 91 was her secret weapon. She loved the verse that said the Lord would rescue her from the snares of her enemies, and that He would protect her against incurable and deadly diseases.

I followed in her footsteps, putting my faith not in a religion per se, but in my spiritual connection with my Maker. Who am I? I am the product of my childhood . . . the product of the environment that shaped and molded me. I am a French teacher responsible to teach French to kindergarteners and middle-schoolers.

What I went through in the educational system in Haiti, where I was punished for not memorizing history and grammar rules, prepared me to become a patient teacher who understands that each student may be carrying a familial burden that can potentially impact their learning. Many parents have kindly revealed to me how much they appreciate my patience with their children. Others have shared with me that they truly believed I was a godsend for the school, specifically for their children.

In the 2016-2017 school year, the mother of one of my former students emailed me and revealed to me that she considers me an answer to her prayers. I found her email to be a divine confirmation, because prior to being hired at the private school, and as I was still completing my master's degree at the university of Alabama in Tuscaloosa, I had prayed and asked the Lord to find me a good school that would accept me as their French teacher. Thus, I smiled when I heard and read such kind words toward me as a French teacher.

I knew that it was only the Lord who promoted my résumé and placed me at this private school. I smiled, recognizing that the Lord worked it all out. He used my horrible childhood to prepare me for a glorious career in teaching. Not only am I a French teacher, but I am also a pastor, preacher, motivational speaker, and author who seeks opportunities to encourage and inspire. What I went through in my childhood has prepared me to minister to a wide range of people who are suffering.

There is a woman in a Haitian church in Huntsville who, as I write this paragraph, suffers from epilepsy. I have been praying with her for at least four years now, asking the Lord to heal her and restore her soul just as it was done for my mother. It pains me to see the woman suffer so much. It hurts my heart to hear her say, "Maladi a te pran'm ankò wi, ma'p tàn gran mèt la," which means, "I had another seizure, but I am waiting on the Lord to heal me."

I will never stop praying for her and with her as much I can until the seizures stop, which I know from experience will stop. My mother's sickness and constant depression gave me a compassionate heart for those who suffer around me and in the world. As a direct result of my childhood, I minister to young people in Florida (and everywhere else when I am invited) to encourage everyone, especially young adults, to embrace their life no matter the circumstances, and no matter their lugubrious past.

My past made me who I am today. My experiences shaped my world view in a positive light, and I am here to plead with you to reinterpret your childhood experiences and use them in a positive way to impact your world.

When I become discouraged, pondering on the racial tension in the US and the way black men and women are being killed in the streets of America, when I start to feel helpless and trapped in an unjust judicial system, when I become disheartened at the way some police officers are unjustly allowing their dogs to chew on their black victims, when I know that it could very well be my turn as an innocent black man caught in the wrong place at the wrong time, I find hope in the knowledge that my mother's Gran Mèt, who is now my Gran Mèt, with the help of God-fearing Americans, will spare my life in the same manner that He spared my mother's.

Who am I today? I am a father to my daughter, Robyn. I pledge to strive daily to provide my precious daughter and her soon-to-come sibling, Layla Rose, with a great, fun, joyous, and unforgettable childhood. I have worked and will continue to work two to three jobs like my father did when he first came to Miami. I will continue to teach French and Haitian Creole. I will continue to tutor, preach, and give motivational speeches for as long as the Lord gives me those opportunities, which also enables me to be able to finance my children's future.

However, if my children are destined to have a horrible childhood like I did so that they may serve a greater purpose than my selfish desires to shelter them—if they came to life to save others through their childhood stories—I will not be able to abort their life purpose. I pray that it pleases the Lord to spare my faint heart from seeing my babies suffer.

Who am I? I am a husband to my beautiful and caring wife, LaQueena. We have decided to combine our childhood experiences and different background knowledge to shape the life of our children and that of many others that we plan to adopt and raise in the future. I know that the Lord will give us the funds and will find us some orphans to influence and raise. We plan to be a blessing to some of the many abandoned Haitian orphans who live in the streets, and who have nobody to care for them. As a matter of fact, my uncle Wilfride and I are working to find a location in Haiti to start sheltering and taking care of a few unfortunate children. We want to be God's angels to the "least of these," feeding, sheltering, clothing, educating, and nurturing them until they are ready to go out and fulfill their purpose by meeting the needs of others.

Who am I? I am the son of my mother, Suzette, and father, Zachari, whose pictures are in this book. They have tried their best to give me a good life. Their stories helped me realize that no matter how well intended I could be toward raising children, things can still turn for the worst.

Who am I? I am a child of God sent to this world for a purpose; primarily to become aware of my maker, and secondarily, to realize what the Lord purposed me to accomplish in the world.

Who am I? I am somebody who has embraced his life no matter the pain endured in the past, no matter the betrayal of family members, and no matter the loneliness. My past is my foundation and not my barrier in life. My past is my ticket to an exciting new life voyage. My past is my password to unlock my purpose. What I considered to be my horrible childhood is, in fact, spring wires set in place to propel me to my purpose and destiny. I hope that my childhood stories did not depress you, but ratter encouraged you to consider your life as a blessing, and to embrace every part of it.

Continue to indulge me as I share with you several stories that I have either read or heard. My goal is to encourage you to reflect on your own life and consider your challenges. I pray that the following stories will motivate you and inform your heart. As you read the stories and the way I interpret them, think of a person who might benefit from the life lessons they teach, and the secrets they reveal. You never know, but one of your life's purposes might be to prevent a friend or coworker from committing suicide.

So far, I have made a clear case in this book for embracing

one's life, and against doing otherwise. Read on to the next stories while actively listening to your inner voice.

My first graduation ceremony in Haiti

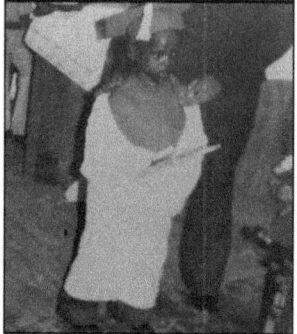

Simone (she saved my mother in the kitchen) with her daughter Widline

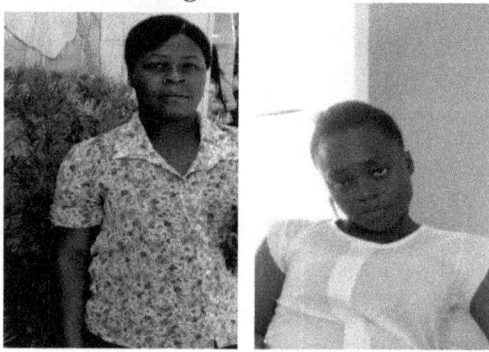

My two lovely daughters. My half-sister Rose and niece Gia

My youngest sister Frandeline   My sister Rodeline

My uncle Wilfride

Chapter 5
Other Interesting Childhood Stories

I have heard many childhood stories that sounded more complicated than what I went through growing up. It is true that the devil is real in Haiti (Ayiti). Not because of Voodoo, but because many Haitians and foreigners take advantage of the defenseless; hurting little children such as the Saint-Anise of the society, and the little orphans. Evil men and women finance civil and economic unrests, thus keeping the country on her knees. The devil is real in Haiti, not only because of a few individuals who use witchcraft to take revenge on those who trespass against them, but also because many criminals get away with their crimes.

The devil is also real in the United States. There are several secret societies and satanic temples. The devil is not only real in the States because of rituals that involve hurting people, but because of the highly organized and planned crimes perpetuated against humanity. The intentional creation of diseases, natural disasters, marginalization of specific groups of people, child prostitution, poisoning food, water and the air are all considered the works of the devil. To me, a father who finds pleasure in sexually abusing his own children becomes the personification of the devil. Unfortunately, there are too many reported cases of this type of crime against children.

I heard the story of a young girl who grew up in a home where her father started molesting her at a very young age. She claimed that as far as she can remember, and when she became aware of herself, she noticed and realized that her father was touching her the wrong way. She sadly reported that it continued as she grew older, and the molestation became regular rape. She explained that as a child, she could not understand why her own father would make her feel so dirty. She felt like she was an adult living in a child's body. She had been forced to take part in things that little children should never even watch, let alone experience.

The effect of her "unfortunate" childhood produced several failed relationships. She was psychologically and sexually damaged. She became bitter and grew up angry. She felt like her bad experience at home had forced her to prematurely grow up.

As she grew older, she began to understand that she could use her past to minister to other children who could be facing the same trauma at home. She made it her life's goal to meet the needs of other women who might be in the closet with a childhood that they considered shameful. She could have become a prostitute, a drug addict, or a serial killer, but that little girl, who is now over 70 years old, decided that she would reinterpret what she went through in her childhood, and turn what the devil meant for evil into a counseling and preaching ministry.

She spent decades teaching little girls to embrace their life no matter the circumstances. Today, she is an author, motivational speaker, a proud mother, and wife of a good man who loves her despite her past. This woman is a role model. She has forgiven her father for his sins against her. She even took care of him before he passed away. What a godly example!

If she could find a lasting relationship after all that she endured—if it was possible for her to forgive her father and even take care of he who oppressed her—I am persuaded that you, too, will find whatever your childhood stole from you.

After what the first man in her life did to her, the way he usurped her young soul and violated her flesh, she should have been single for the rest of her life. Her soul should have been shattered in thousands of pieces. Somehow, as in Psalms 23, the Lord restored her soul and placed a garnished table before her in the presence of her father, her abuser. He gave her back the years that were stolen from her.

As of the year 2017, she has written about 15 inspirational books, and has a net worth of 25 million dollars. She is the personification of someone who has embraced her life and fulfilled her purpose in life.

This woman has met many needs in her community and worldwide. I only learned about her story from the impact her ministry and books have had on my wife. My wife did not only watch this woman's broadcasts, but she made me drive her to Birmingham—we were living in Huntsville, Alabama at the time—to attend one of her live conferences. Prior to her conference in Birmingham, I had never been at a live event in a stadium where people came to listen to a minister. She was phenomenal, reaching both the men and the women who attended her conferences. Her message was too powerful for one event, so she made available several of her books that filled the lobby area of the stadium.

The lines to purchase her books were extremely long, but people, including my family, were happy to wait. I believe that the same Lord who restored the woman's soul prospered her, and most importantly, used her to inspire others to be restored and to prosper . . . and He will use you as well.

I cannot explain why the Lord allows His children to suffer in this world. I may never be able to explain why children are still being exploited around the world. But one thing I am commissioned to share with you today is that you must embrace your life no matter what you went through in your childhood. There is always a purpose to your suffering, and if you can find the strength to embrace your life no matter the circumstances, you will be able to make a powerful impact on your world.

Many abused women could have chosen to live their life in depression, but instead, they chose to positively use what they went through in their childhood to become influential and powerful women. They have become powerful mothers who continue to supply the world with caring and godly children who will uplift their generation.

In 2014, while I lived in Huntsville, Alabama, I went to a Seventh-day Adventist church, Madison Mission. It was a regular Saturday weekly worship service. The entire congregation was on the brink of tears listening to the testimony of a young, white male who had suffered unbearably during his childhood at the hands of his own father. His story was extremely painful to listen to, for the simple fact that his father prostituted him to other older men. I did not want to believe what I was hearing, because the story was not making any sense to me. I could not understand why his father would not protect and love him as nature and instinct would have him do. Even as I write this paragraph, I still cannot imagine a father treating his son in that manner; it is such an aberration to me.

The man claimed that his father physically and sexually abused him. As a child, it hurt him the most to learn that his father did not love him. I am sure as a boy he kept asking himself what it was that he must do to make his father love him. He probably kept thinking that things were going to improve. Unfortunately for him, things got worse until he was old enough to move out of the house. He said that he began to use drugs to drown his pain, but praise be to the Creator of life, he accepted a faith system that helped him in ways that the drugs could not. Jesus, he claimed, helped him carry his childhood burdens, and became his Lord and savior.

Once Jesus found him, He cleaned him psychologically and spiritually. Now that man is a traveling evangelist who is invited all over the map to let the entire world know that his childhood mess became his inspiring message to suffering children in adult bodies.

The man could have easily chosen to continue to abuse drugs. He could have chosen to be mad at the world and at the Creator Himself, but instead, he reinterpreted his childhood in the light of the Word of God. What the devil, through his human father, meant to destroy him, only made him stronger and gave him a more powerful testimony out of his life's tests to share with the rest of the suffering world. He has been to hell and back, and now he is more than qualified to minister to children, young adults, adults, and anybody else who will listen to his story.

I cannot talk about his accomplishments, because I do not recall his name. I do not know if he has written books, or if he has started a foundation. But one thing I do know is that his testimony reached his listeners, and certainly motivated them to embrace their life.

I heard someone say that things could always be worse, and that "dèyè mòn gen mòn," which means there are higher mountains behind the mountains that ours eyes can see. Basically, my childhood mountains were not the highest amongst the world's mountainous childhood experiences. Some children in the same neighborhood might have had it worse than me, as well as the woman or the man in the previous stories. Therefore, we must embrace our life, because it could have been worse.

Are you still reading? Are you asking yourself why I am sharing such sad stories? Are you saying that it is enough, and that you do not need any more proof? That every life is worth embracing? Please continue to indulge me, for I just want to make sure that by the end of this book, you make a firm decision to embrace your life no matter the circumstances. I just want you to compare your life story with the stories that I am purposely sharing with you, and ask yourself, "If those people can reinterpret their childhood nightmares and turn them into a ministry, a book, or a career to help build other broken people around the world, what is stopping you from doing the same thing?" You never know; your childhood story may become the next bestseller. God may have somebody out there who is willing to put your childhood story into an inspirational movie for the world to see, thus impacting many families around the world that you probably would never meet in a lifetime.

I am probably never going to meet you in person, and that

is okay, because I already feel fulfilled and blessed to have ministered to your soul thus far. Please tarry with me for a little while as I share a few more stories to encourage you to embrace your life no matter the circumstances.

It is crucial that you do so, for not only does your wellbeing depend on it, but that of your entire family as well. You will do it for your children's wellbeing, and ultimately for the community at large. If you do not want it for yourself, think about the purpose that the Creator hid in you, and the people He has already assigned you to help. There is a need out there that is waiting for you to meet it. There is a book that only you are inspired to write because of your unique childhood experience. There is an app that only you can create to meet the need that only you had the vision to identify. When you embrace your life, you eventually meet some needs.

You have probably already read the story of Ben Carson, who grew up in a house where his father was absent, and who became one of the first neurosurgeons to successfully separate conjoined twins. If you have already read his story, please allow me to share with you my interpretation of his childhood.

I am sure growing up in his neighborhood was not easy for a black child with no role model, and whose mother worked as hard as a slave to provide for him and his brother. Perhaps there were times when his mother would come home tired, with no strength to cook dinner. I am certain that there were times when they could not afford some nice pair of shoes, or good name-brand clothes for school. I cannot imagine how hard it was during Christmas time, but somehow, Ben Carson became a famous black neurosurgeon in America, and in 2015-2016, he ran for the presidency of one of the most powerful countries in the world.

If Ben Carson had allowed his past to dictate his future, he would have never become an expert in the art of separating conjoined twins, and thus blessing two children with a normal life on this planet. If Ben's mother had not embraced her hard life and worked hard at preparing her children, if she was always so depressed that she could not help her two boys, life could have been different for Ben and his brother in America.

Although I believe that many black men are systematically marginalized in the United States and around the European world, and even in their own land in the African continent, I also believe that the US is the sole country in the West that gives great economic opportunities to men and women of African descent, as well as other minority groups. I have no faith in its justice system, but I have faith in the fact that in America, anyone can go from being dirt poor to being wealthy if they embrace their life and meet a need.

Ben Carson embraced his childhood and became a famous surgeon at the Johns Hopkins hospital on September 6, 1987. There were times when he was growing up that he struggled in school, and that his young mother at the time began decreasing his television time and increasing his study time. Although his mother was his rock and his guide, Ben had to help raise his younger brother while his mother worked two to three jobs to support them financially. I saw in a documentary on his life that he had anger issues as a child, and that he used to read Bible verses to help calm his nerves. He might not have known that he was embracing his life without a father, his life with an overworked mother, his life with academic challenges while striving to change his situation and that of his mother, but that is exactly what he did.

Ben was born for the specific purpose to be the neurosurgeon who led a seventy-member surgical team and separated the German twins. He was born to write the best-seller, Gifted Hands, and have a movie made about his life. How was it possible for a man whose parents were divorced, and whose mother only had a third-grade education and married a polygamist at 13 years of age? How was it possible for Ben Carson to become so famous from a mother who really could not read, and was a servant? How was it possible for a man who was the class dummy in the fourth and fifth grade to become a motivational speaker who lectures and encourages young people about using their brain?

The answer is quite simple; it is the theme of this book. He and his mother embraced their situations and made the best out of them. Let us embrace our life and bless someone else in doing so.

Like myself, Joyce Meyer, and Ben Carson, you have got to reinterpret your childhood. Make a positive impact on your world and those who live in it. Your life's story is important; it is the foundation of a new ministry, a new business, a new cure, new methodologies, new aspirations, new perspectives, and new psychological wings to fly above life's challenges. As we know, those challenges could be familial, societal, cultural, physical, spiritual, and financial. If we embrace our life no matter which of those challenges we may have faced or we are currently facing, the Creator will use us to bless other people and keep them from going through what we went through. We were born to commune with our Creator vertically, and minister to one another horizontally. Let us be the hands, feet, mouth, eyes, and ears of God in our needy world.

Allow me to share one more American success childhood story with you. I am thinking about the story of the well-known TD Jakes. Most people in America and around the world who have had access to a television set has seen or heard him preach. He does such an amazing job at preaching that many people predicted that he would be the next Billy Graham. I personally disagree and think that he is already bigger than Billy Graham. He is such a powerful preacher, motivational speaker, and author, that people from all around the world travel to come and hear him speak. He is so well-spoken that he can hold a crowd captive by every word that comes out of his mouth. He often states that his mission is to minister to broken people, especially women. Out of that mission, his yearly stadium gathering was birthed, where thousands of men and women come to hear a message about "woman thou art loose."

His great sermons have not only ministered to women, but also to men all over the world. I have been personally blessed and encouraged by his ministry. Although I prefer his 1996 through 2001 sermons, I enjoy listening to the way he applies Bible verses to real life challenges. I have been addicted to his sermons on YouTube since 2001, and I have learned plenty of life's principles from his hermeneutical approach of the Bible.

What is interesting about TD Jake's story is that he grew up with a speech problem. It is interesting that he became a famous preacher, yet he could not speak clearly. He said that his hands used to shake uncontrollably to the point where he could not hold a microphone to speak. He claimed, as a little boy, to have been bullied at school and beat up at the bus stop. He did not grow up in a rich family. Consequently, he told of his childhood stories with his siblings eating peanut butter and jelly sandwiches. His English teacher told him that his writing was not good enough, but somehow TD Jakes has written at least seven bestsellers.

His books and DVDs are sold around the world. He is the founder of the Potter's House Ministry, and he has hired hundreds of people in the Dallas, Texas area. When he first started his church, he struggled for membership and had to work a side job to support it financially. He confessed that he could not afford a church staff, and that sometimes he had to put his entire paycheck in the offering plate.

Having embraced his childhood and embraced his calling, he toiled day and night, but was successful in the end. His church in Virginia grew from 100 members to 300 members. He then moved to Dallas, Texas and became the senior pastor of a congregation of 30,000 members. He was born to meet a need. He was born to minister to me and the millions of other young people.

In my opinion, he is the best and the greatest preacher in my lifetime. How did he do it? He did not allow his past to hinder his future and keep him captive. He did not allow his tormentors, teachers, and physical challenges to make him suicidal, depressed, or become a drug addict. This man is a prime example of somebody who uses his stories to his advantage. As a matter of fact, he said in one of his video sermons that "nothing you have been through will be lost." I believe he meant that our past experiences can be recycled to bless ourselves and others.

For instance, when TD Jakes mentioned that he once had a speech impediment, he encouraged his listeners who could have been dealing with speech problems as well. When he talked about how he was bullied at the bus stop as a child, he encouraged some of his listeners who could be dealing with bullying. When he talked about his English teacher who said that he could not write, he encouraged other people who aspired to write and share their story with the world despite their academic difficulties. When he preached about Jesus showing His wounded hands to His disciples, he encouraged me and his listeners to reveal to others our scars. Showing others your childhood scars will minister to them and help them to see the real you.

If TD Jakes can reinterpret all that he went through, why can't you do the same thing? I believe that you can. Like former president Barack Obama, "Yes, we can" embrace our wounds, embrace our childhood, and embrace our life to benefit others.

What you went through must be reinterpreted, or else you are robbing the world of your contribution, your ministry, your gift, your talent, and your testimony. Your wounds are your badge of honor. Do not hide them.

The world needs you, so do not deny it your service; do not destroy the blessing that is hidden in your childhood story; do not deprive us of your part of life's puzzle. I am pleading with you on behalf of the rest of the world to share with us your story. Encourage us with your wounds, and uplift us with your personal challenges. We all need to hear your story. Please use whatever means necessary—radio, television, books and social media—to get your story out there and change the world. Everyone who has had a horrible experience and turned it into an uplifting story has successfully embraced life no matter the circumstances.

Enough American inspirational stories for now. The following is a story that I heard growing up in Haiti. It had a real impact on me, and it forced me to reflect on the possibility that life can certainly be aborted, especially after hearing it told at a church, which I thought was the place where God breathed life into His believers and not death.

As a child, I unrealistically thought we live, have fun, eat, and play forever. Death and separation from my family never entered my mind until my father migrated to the United States, and seeing my mother constantly sick. It became real to me the morning that my mother said, "I was up all night keeping you from killing yourself."

She claimed that I was under a malevolent psychic influence that aimed at cutting my life short. That revelation shattered my childish and naïve perspective about life. I pray and hope that this story is inspirational enough to motivate you, and may it persuade you to embrace your life no matter the circumstances.

Growing up in Haiti, I heard a Haitian preacher share a testimony that I still remember vividly as if I'd just heard it a few minutes ago. The pastor said that his mother revealed to him something that shattered his childhood perspective on life. At first, it did not make any sense to him, but as he grew older, he confessed that he understood it a little bit better. His mother explained to him that when he was in her womb, she was in a world of trouble, because it was not acceptable for a teenager to be pregnant outside of marriage.

Contrary to popular belief, Haitian parents abhor the idea of their daughters becoming pregnant out of wedlock. It is not acceptable in the Haitian culture, and it is a disgrace for families who are fanatically religious. Haitian parents hate it with a passion when their little girls bring "shame" on their family by having an "illegitimate" child. Consequently, in retaliation for such public embarrassment, most parents either force their daughters to marry the father of their unborn child, or put their daughters out of the house.

Their intentions are to teach the child a lesson, and to prove to their neighbors, church family, and their immediate family members that they do not condone their daughters' choice of "ruining" their life in that manner. Delicate situations of that sort force the confused, pregnant children to either have an unfortunate abortion, or attempt to raise and nurture a baby without the family's financial and physical support.

The pastor explained that his mother was in an unpleasant predicament. She could not get married, because the family of the boy did not want to give their consent. She wanted to continue with her education and she did not want to be banished from her parents' home. Thus, she decided that she would force herself to have a miscarriage.

She attempted everything she could possibly think of, but her baby boy refused to be aborted. The pastor was very emotional as he shared his testimony with the church. He said that his mother tried to jump down a few stairs to miscarry him, but God would not let him die in her womb. No matter how she attempted to hurt him, he miraculously survived every time.

His story made him famous in the Seventh-day Adventist Church in Port-au-Prince, Haiti. Everyone expected him to cry because he was furious; his own mother attempted to steal his life. He did cry, but fury was not the cause of his tears. Most of us would have been depressed knowing that we were an unwanted child, or that we were an accident. In fact, I have heard stories of people who refuse to forgive their parents for giving them up for adoption. This pastor was crying while telling his story because he was amazed that even in the womb of his mother, and when he was not intellectually aware of himself, the Creator was his "refuge and strength, a very present help in trouble."

He was grateful that his life was spared, therefore he reinterpreted what almost happened to him as proof that the Lord chose him to be a minister to His people. He could have become bitter about the fact that his mother tried several times to abort him. He could have chosen to hate his mother and complain that he was not wanted. Instead, he chose to use his unfortunate situation and minister to others. He decided that he would use that story to encourage men and women who may have felt betrayed by their parents. The Bible says, and I paraphrase, "God will take care of His children even when their parents abandon them."

This preacher left a lasting impact on my life as a boy, and now you are reaping the benefits. Had the pastor hid his story and not shared it to purposely edify his listeners, I would not have been so impacted and invigorated by it. Using his life story, I am now writing to encourage anyone who would read what the Creator has placed in me to share with the world.

This pastor's life story is a ministry to all the so-called unwanted children of the world. Were you an unwanted child? Do you know a neighbor, classmate, church member, or coworker who was an unwanted child? Beware of your unwanted self; you might be destined to meet a great need at some point in your life.

Please feel free to share any of the testimonies in this book. Do not forget to remind your listeners to embrace their life no matter the circumstances.

There is a well-known biblical story that I am going to share with you. It is about a boy named Joseph who was born and raised in a dysfunctional and supposedly godly household. I believe that you can benefit from the story even if you are not a Bible believing Christian. The life's principles extracted from this story could be helpful to anyone regardless of their religious affiliation or belief system. I implore you to stay with me a little while longer as I try to extract some of the golden wisdom hidden beneath the surface of this story, and reiterate the absolute necessity of embracing the childhood and life you were given when you came to this corrupted world.

None of us had the option of choosing our childhood, and ultimately our life. We must embrace what we have been given and reinterpret it to bless somebody else. The following Bible verse is the foundation, or the cornerstone, upon which this entire book is based. It helped me realize that none can embrace life no matter the circumstances unless he or she can say with Joseph to a father, a pastor, a police officer, a judge, a brother, a mother, a sister, a family member, a neighbor, a coworker, or a classmate, "You intended to hurt me, but God used it for good, not just to benefit me, but to also benefit others."

This text is so powerful and rich, that before diving into it, I will ask you a few questions, and share with you my interpretation of the relevant story of an American goddess named Anarcha. Although the story of Joseph is great, I believe that the story of Anarcha will richly bless you, and it will encourage you to live despite your challenges.

Has your spouse hurt you badly? Have your parents betrayed you? Has your pastor or church member disappointed you? Have your siblings mistreated you? Have you been wronged by the justice system? Have you been brutalized by a "rotten apple" police officer?

As an officer of the law, have you been falsely accused by a citizen or by your department? Have your neighbors been unfair to you? Have you been persecuted for speaking out against systematic injustice? What about your coworkers; have they made your job harder? Have you been a victim of medical malpractice? Have you been innocently incarcerated and hurt? Whatever you may have endured, whoever may have intended to hurt you meant it for evil. But destiny wanted to use the same undesirable situation for good, and to meet a need in the greater community.

I do not pretend to understand why God allows us to hurt and abuse one another, but I believe that He uses every single one of our mistakes to make them serve His purpose for our good. In that light, I interpret every evil action as a potential tool in the hands of the divine.

Dr. Sims atrocities against black women in the South were repulsive. Could God have used his evil and filthy hands for the good of the greater community? Could the disheartening and endless tears of his victims be used as a libation for generations of women to come? Whatever the correct answer may be, destiny has already taken care of it . . . or it will surely take care of it. Do not think for a second that I approve any of the evil actions of Sims, the medical witch doctor. In fact, I strongly condemn what Dr. J. Marion Sims did to poor and defenseless black female slaves in his days.

He was known to have performed repeated, excruciatingly painful surgeries on black women without anesthesia. According to a 2006 Washington post article, a black woman named Anarcha Wescott endured 30 surgeries without any anesthesia. The savage and soulless doctor might have intended to selfishly improve gynecology using the living soul of another human being. The poor Anarcha might have prayed and begged the Lord to deliver her from the repeated mutilation of her already wounded and martyred flesh, but God, in His omnipotence and omniscience, allowed it to serve a greater purpose.

I sincerely believe that God has used her unfortunate situation to bring to light the evil of racism. Maybe God has not yet used her torture to save any life, or maybe He has already used her pain to improve the science of gynecology. I am not sure what the Lord did or what He will do, I do not know why in His omnipresence He did not strike dead the evil doctor. One thing of which I am certain, Anarcha's story will meet a great need at some point in our pitiful existence . . . if it hasn't already done so.

Anarcha, and the many other black women who were subjugated by the merciless hands of Dr. Sims and his heartless co-conspirators, should always be remembered and venerated. In fact, Anarcha is known as the mother of gynecology by many who understand the sacrificial intrusion of her sacred life-given organ. Her story of suffering is not different from your story of pain. The level of pain you have experienced might not have been as unbearable as Anarcha's level of pain, but we are all part of a suffering, heartless humanity.

Joseph said in Genesis 50:20 to his blood relatives who made him suffer, "You intended to harm me, but God intended it for good to accomplish what is now being done, the saving of many people's life."

If you have never read or heard the story of Joseph, the above quotation is a direct reference to what he said to his brothers who made his life miserable when he was a little boy. If I can digress a little bit, I want to share with you the background of the story of Joseph so that you may get the best possible lessons out of it, the same way I did.

I have learned, through reading the ancestry of Joseph and digging in his past, that the Creator meticulously planned each of our lives. In His omniscience, He knows that we have free will and that we will exercise it according to our own heart's desire. This truth is revealed in the life of Joseph. His past, which is the life of his parents, including his childhood, teaches important lessons that should not be ignored. From it, I have learned that one should never sweep his or her past under a rug, attempting to forget or erase it. Instead, one should embrace his or her past and use it as a navigation system for the future.

Chapter 6
Joseph's Interesting Childhood

It is written in the Bible that Joseph was the son of Jacob, grandson of Isaac, and great grandson of Abraham. You may be asking yourself about the relevance of this information, but I think that it is important for us to establish the fact that Joseph grew up in a totally dysfunctional family. Both his great grandfather Abraham and grandfather Isaac were unstable men who kept moving from place to place, with a rich heritage of family drama. His own father, Jacob, prior to settling on the land of Canaan with all his children, ran away from home because he lied to his blind father, Isaac, and stole his brother's birthright and went in hiding at his uncle's house for nearly 21 years.

Have you had to run away from home to escape the wrath of a sibling or parent? If so, be encouraged! If God was still with Jacob when he ran away from home, He was and will also be with you away from your family.

Have your children left your safety net prematurely? Do not worry. Although it is easier said than done, do not panic. The Creator will surely provide for your lost family members, for each of them has a purpose.

I am sure that Jacob's parents worried about him. I am certain that they missed him, but God took good care of him. Jacob went to live with a family member because he could not get along with his twin brother. Common sense says that if you cannot live peacefully with your own brother, there is a possibility that life with an uncle or another family member may not be that peaceful.

One would think that once Jacob arrived at his uncle Laban's house that he would have found peace and would have been able to start his life anew. That was not the case, because the Bible tells us that Joseph's father had to run away once again from his uncle's farm to settle in the land of Canaan. His uncle did not care for him like he cared for his own children. We should all love our siblings, but I do not think that we should trust our children blindly to their care.

My mother knows a Haitian proverb that she quotes all the time: "Se mèt afè k' okipe afè." It means that an owner will always take good care of his or her belongings better than someone who is watching over it temporarily. In other words, no one can take care of your children better than you. My mother knows another Haitian proverb that says: "Pa'ou se pa'ou." It means "what is yours is yours."

An uncle will never replace a father, and an aunt can never replace a mother. That is why we should keep a close eye on our children when we allow a family member to watch over them.

I knew a little girl in Haiti who was left in the care of her aunt because her mother lived in the countryside, and she had no money to feed or educate her. Her aunt's house was a few feet away from mine. The first week when she arrived at her aunt's home, her cousins were happy to have her around. They all played together and lived like good relatives. Unfortunately, after the second week, the little girl became the housekeeper who cleaned up after everyone. She had to fetch water daily before dawn, and take care of her younger and older cousins. She was mistreated by her aunt and cousins. Sometimes they did not even feed her. They would beat her, and the little devils would mercilessly make fun of her.

In Haiti, we did not have a child protective service back when I was a child, and consequently, the little girl was left to the mercy of her heartless aunt. When we realized that her aunt was not interested in the wellbeing of her own niece, we decided to give the little girl some money and encouraged her to return home to her mother. One day, she escaped and we were very happy that she never came back.

Family members do not always take good care of one

another, but God will always make a way out for His children. Jacob had to escape when his uncle Laban was away on business. Laban would have murdered him if God had not intervened and protected him. The problem was that Jacob's uncle did not play fair with him, just as Jacob had not played fair with his father, Isaac, and brother, Esau. Laban exploited Jacob's youthful strength and selfishly made him labor to acquire more wealth. This stunning revelation from Josephs' past is remarkable when one considers the way Joseph's relationships with his siblings and acquaintances was going to mirror that of his father.

For this reason, I found it interesting that Genesis chapter 37 starts by mentioning that Jacob dwelled, or settled, in the land where his father and grandfather were strangers. The fact that Jacob dwelled where his father was a stranger is symbolic to me. I interpret it and understand it to mean that many of us will have to deal with some of the same things our parents dealt with growing up; thus, the lying and exploitation that crossed several generations. We can even take it further and say that our fathers were strangers to the new technologies that we have today, but we are settled and very comfortable using them.

We must remember that our generation is going to be a stranger to where the next generation will go or what it will have to face. That is why I found it fascinating that Jacob dwelled in the land wherein his father was a stranger, and later, Joseph's children dwelled in a land wherein their father was a stranger.

Ironically, I am currently living and dwelling in an American land where my father was a stranger some decades ago. I am not working to provide for a wife and children living in Haiti in the same manner my father did in the early 80s when he first moved to Miami and left us in Port-au-Prince. But I am settled here and I am working like a slave to provide for my wife and children whom I have left in Huntsville, Alabama while working in Birmingham.

The wisdom in this interpretation is that we must be careful in what we do, and how we carry ourselves around our children. They will naturally follow our trails as parents, therefore, we must be intentional about setting up good pathways for them. It starts with embracing life no matter the circumstances, and doing our best with what we have while striving for better. We must avoid complaining about our past, and, for the sake of our children, we must refrain from blaming everybody else for our current situations. We should try our best to create peaceful homes and work hard at keeping discord at bay. Dysfunctional homes might create dysfunctional children who will repeat the cycle. Let us work to improve the future of our children.

Joseph's father, Jacob, is a good example of a man who grew up in a dysfunctional home. He was clearly not the favorite of his father, but the favorite of his mother. This is a man who conspired with his cunning mother and took by trickery the blessing of his father, which was intended for his older brother by birthright. Jacob tricked both his father and his older brother, because he refused to embrace the life he was given and decided that he would play God and take by force a different life than that which was given to him.

It is very dangerous to improve one's self at the detriment of others. If you must lie to steal a blessing, you will most likely hurt someone else. If our purpose in life is to meet the need of someone else, then being a trickster is not embracing life. Jacob hurt his twin brother and broke his father's heart. Jacob was, in turn, tricked by his own uncle and later he was tricked by his sons in the alleged murder of their younger brother, Joseph.

If Jacob had embraced his life no matter what was happening at home in his childhood, he would have avoided many of the calamities that came upon him and his children. I found the same to be true for Isaac and Abraham.

Unfortunately, their mistakes became pathways for their children to follow, and in which they were going to settle.

Abraham lied about his wife and said that she was his sister. Although she was truly his half-sister, his intention was to save and protect himself. His lie placed his wife in danger of rape and abuse from the lustful men who were looking at her with wishful desires in their hearts. Isaac, his son, did the exact same thing in the exact same situation. He lied about his wife and said that she was his sister. He wanted to protect his life, and thus placed his wife in the same danger that Abraham had placed his.

Jacob appeared to be lucky in the sense that he did not have to lie about his wife to save his life, but he had to marry two sisters who despised and competed against each other. They both forced Jacob to sleep with their female servant to have children on their behalf. Originally, Jacob only loved the youngest sister, who was named Rachel. His uncle promised that he would allow him to marry her if, and only if, he agreed to work seven years to earn her.

Seven years later, his uncle tricked him and gave him the wrong wife, Rachel's older sister Leah, whom Jacob did not love. Jacob was angry and embarrassed, but because he had abundant love for Rachel, he agreed to work an additional seven long years in order to finally marry his true love. The depth of his love for Rachel was remarkable, nevertheless, he was reaping what he had previously sown.

The skilled trickster was finally tricked, the crafty liar was disappointingly lied to, the expert deceiver was greatly deceived, and the prankster was shamefully pranked. Jacob's turbulent life should teach us to be careful how we treat one another, not only to prevent bad karma, but most importantly, because we were born for the benefit of each other. We can never be sure about many things in life, but we know through experience that what goes around does seem to come back around.

Jacob thought all he was doing was outsmarting his twin brother; he was over withdrawing his "peace" account, or he was signing a bad check for his future. When we exploit one another, we exploit ourselves. What we do today—the way we treat people now—will have a ripple effect on the community at large, and it will affect our future experiences at some level. So, let us make every effort necessary to be honest in our approach to the future.

Jacob coveted his twin brother's birth right, which guaranteed Esau a greater portion of the family's inheritance. Jacob did well to think about his future, but taking advantage of his brother to gain a better future was unacceptably wrong.

We can see clearly in the story of Jacob, the father of Joseph, that there are repercussions for our actions, and that there is always a reaction to every action. I was curious to see what was going to happen to Jacob's mother, the woman who helped put the plan together to trick both her son and her husband. Rebecca did most of the planning for Jacob, while Esau was out hunting to prepare his father's favorite meal.

Esau was a hairy boy, but Jacob was not. Rebecca helped Jacob with a special handmade costume that was designed to fool her blind husband into thinking that he was touching the skin of Esau. She also helped Jacob with her husband's favorite meal to guarantee the successful transfer of his blessings to Jacob before the return of Esau from hunting. We need to remember that she was the mother of the twins, and that she was supposed to love them both equally.

The first time I heard this story at a church in Haiti, I asked myself why she favored one son over the other. I still wonder what she said to Esau when he came back from hunting and realized that Jacob had stolen his blessing. What did she say to console Esau when he became depressed? Did she experience any guilt? Did she confess to him that she was an accomplice? Did she ever reveal to her husband, Isaac, that it was her idea, and that she advised Jacob to run away from home with his blessing?

After Jacob left the home of his parents, the Bible ceased to talk about his mother, and thus her story ended ambiguously. I had many questions relative to her life after

Jacob left. I asked myself how her actions might have had a role on her grandson, Joseph's future. Was Joseph's pain a direct result of his grandmother's sneaky actions? Did she ever pay for what she conspired to do? Apart from losing her favorite son, Jacob, and her brother, Laban, mistreating and exploiting her son, did she personally suffer or pay for her actions? Did Jacob carry the entire load alone?

I am not sure if an exegetical study of the text could answer my pertinent questions, or if you, who might be a theologian, have the answers. With my limited understanding of the matter, I see two different interpretations on the way her story ended. First, embracing my life means to not allow anyone, including my parents, to influence me and to make me usurp someone else's blessing. I never forget that I might be the only one who is punished for my actions regardless of whom conspired with me. Second, I must embrace my life even if I do not see equal justice. I have read stories of black and white young men who committed the same crimes, but one received a lesser sentence than the other. The fact of the matter is that nature has its law, which says that everyone will reap what they sow.

Parents, I believe it is important for us to notice that the way we live our life might influence the way our children live their own. Teaching them to be honest and just should be one of our primary goals. It will be a blessing to their offspring, who will undoubtedly follow in their footsteps. We should be careful to live a righteous life; our main goal should be to help others and not deceive them.

Deception has been around for a long time. Powerful nations have conquered naïve and gullible peoples by deceiving them. Many children were hurt because an adult predator deceived them. Many evil and wicked people intentionally deceive their prey with what looks like a genuine smile.

I find it interesting to reflect on the fact that the biblical narrative starts with the deception of a snake with the sole purpose of seducing an innocent woman, and it concludes the story of humanity with the last book known as the book of Revelation chapter 12 verse 9. It says, and I paraphrase, "An old serpent was thrown down. They call him the devil. He works at deceiving the whole world."

We should, therefore, work hard at meeting a need in our society and not deceiving those for whom we came into the world. If we believe in the biblical stories as God's instruction manual for our life, we should try our best to not be associated with the old serpent, the dragon of revelation who chased the pregnant and vulnerable woman in the wilderness, and who deceived the entire world.

If you want to know who the devil has used and is using on earth, read the pages of history and pay attention to current events. You will learn about the many individuals and systems that have deceived the rest of us. When you deceive to gain an advantage over someone else, you become an enemy who threatens the peace of everyone else.

Embrace your life no matter what, or create more chaos in the family.

One of the many lessons that can be learned from considering Joseph's ancestry is that each generation that refuses to embrace life no matter the circumstances, causes more problems for the next, thus, creating what many call a generational curse. It is very simple to stop generational curses; very simple to stop leaving financial and psychological debts for the next generation. We simply need to make a decision and actively work toward destroying generational curses in our life. If not, we will unwillingly and inevitably transfer it to our children. Before we can effectively destroy a generational curse, we must first identify its source, and then work against it.

Embracing life no matter the circumstances does not mean to stop fighting for a better life. Everyone must come up with a personalized definition of the term "better life." I believe that life becomes better once we have successfully overcome the demons—"bad cards"—that we inherited from our parents, and stop the continual transfer permanently in our lifetime. It is evident that the next generation will have to work just as hard to ensure that no curse is transferred to the generation that follows. We must simply embrace the life that we were given, and make the best out of it without trying to exploit, outsmart, or control anyone.

Our fight is against our circumstances and not against people. In this game of life, the only way to win is to play well the cards given to us, and try our best not to leave a load of bad cards to our children. Many of us suffer from old problems that run through our family. Some of us battle the same demons with which our great grandparents battled. I believe that it is time to conquer those demons; we can conquer them all. Whether it is the demon of alcohol, crack cocaine, heroin, methamphetamine, divorce, pornography, prostitution, sexual, verbal and physical abuse, or racism, I implore you to put your foot down and conquer it. By any means necessary, you need to fight this demon out of your house, out of your family, out of your children, out of your church, your city, your country, and out of your generation.

I was proud of a father who went on television and denounced his son's white supremacist views. His son was one of the torch bearing, hateful men in Charlottesville, Virginia who caused the death of an innocent, white female protestor. What the father did was courageous and encouraging. It gave hope to the rest of the non-white human beings that the curse of racism will one day be destroyed. Apparently, his son did not inherit his racism from him, but I wonder how he became a white supremacist.

We should all be as courageous as this white supremacist father, and confront the curse in our families. Let us do our best to be the one to destroy it. What if there were awards presented to people who destroy generational curses? What if we deify those who create policies to end that which destroy our world? Do not play with your curse; your job is to destroy it. Do not indulge it for any reason; your job is to destroy it. Do not encourage anybody to fall prey to its power. Do not joke about it, but, instead, destroy it.

Do not allow your circumstances or any dysfunctional family affair to ever force you to willingly accept any of those above-mentioned life and generation destroyers. Once you have identified a deceiving, racist, manipulating, raping, substance abuse generational curse in your family, you should do whatever it takes to eliminate it and protect the rest of the community from it. Please allow my vivid imagination to describe them as some of the most violent, flesh-eating, and generation destroyer demons that must be attacked, eradicated, and destroyed before they attack us and destroy our offspring. Let us embrace our life and declare war on our family generational curses.

Perhaps you are asking yourself if the same principles apply to those out there who grew up in a poor neighborhood, and who embraced their situation and sold drugs to become rich and give back to the community. Some of them sponsor a child from a different country with drug money. Some may say, "I have donated prostitution money to help the poor around the world."

On one hand, I personally do not believe, based on the interpretation of the story of Joseph, that we should use a lesser evil for what seems to be a greater good. I believe that selling drugs to help other people, or to get out of poverty, is literally the act of swapping one life for another. Those generational curses affect us in a bad way. They destroy our family and create chaos for the next generation.

I do not think that it is fair to kill one life to redeem another. I think evil is evil no matter how well we dress it, and no matter how well we justify the use of it. I sincerely believe that all we are doing when trying to manipulate evil is creating debt for the next generation to repay, and hardly overcome. That is why I believe that we must embrace our life no matter what, or else we create more chaos for our children, and future generations with which they are going to grapple at some point in life.

On the other hand, who am I to judge what a childhood life becomes? I am only an observer, privy and amazed at the fact that the Creator will use any childhood experience to save and influence lives.

Fathers who refuse to embrace the family that God has given them—and allow themselves to neglect their children and wife for a job, another woman, a church, or anything else—are creating real chaos for everyone. If the family is broken, then the church is broken. If the church is broken, then the community is broken. If the community is broken, then the city is broken. If the city is broken, then the state is broken. If the state is broken, then the country is broken, and ultimately the world is broken.

Fathers, please embrace your life no matter your circumstances. Your children are counting on you, and God is counting on you to keep harmony in the family. Be involved in your children's life. Do not abandon them to the government or the church to raise them for you. Be a presence in their life. You will not regret that precious investment.

Many young boys and girls are being raised in a single parent home without a father. I know partly how they feel based on my own childhood story. Father's Day celebrations must be one of the worst celebrations for those children. How do they handle an entire weekend of television commercials that persuade viewers to purchase a gift or a greeting card to make fathers feel special? How do they interpret the absence of their own father at their birthday party and graduation ceremony? What about the coping mechanism they use for embarrassing class discussions, where students are encouraged to reflect on their parents' involvement in their education, and talk publicly about a favorite family vacation?

Fathers, let us embrace our life in such a way that we do not place our children in compromising and desperate situations where they will be forced to lie and create a story of the "father" they wish they had. Embracing our life as fathers means to assume our responsibilities, and take care of our boys and girls. Taking care of them guarantees that they are not raised by music videos, obscene movies, social media, or their young friends at school. The Creator built our children with a lot of love; let us not turn their innate love into bitterness and hatred because we were absent from their life.

While attending a church service at Agape in Huntsville, Alabama, I heard the testimony of a young Haitian man. He said that his father, for no apparent reason, decided to expel him, forcing him to go live with family members who could barely take care of themselves. The young man testified that he was sad, because his father was the sole parent with the financial means to take care of him.

As a child, he could not understand why his father rejected him. It was not that he was a terrible son; his father was simply preoccupied with less important things than parenting. While listening to my brother's testimony, who was also a father, I realized that he still missed his dad, and wished that their relationship was better. I empathized and identified with his love and need for his father, for I know from experience how deep of a void a father can leave in his children's lives, and how much family chaos a father creates by being absent.

Fathers, let us not put our children out of our homes before the right time, or simply because they are disobedient. When they are ready, they will leave our homes, but it is cruel to send them out into a vicious world ill-prepared. They will be prone to disagree with us, and they might decide to not adhere to our religious beliefs. It is possible that they will try things out that can be detrimental to their health and wellbeing. But let us not force them to be homeless because they choose a sexual orientation with which we disagree. We will not abandon them should they decide to pick their own career and not the ones that we chose for them. Embracing our life and not creating chaos in the family means to support, parent, protect, teach, guide, help, and enable our children as much as possible.

Additionally, we should intentionally turn our phones, televisions, computers, and other electronic devices off so that we can spend quality time with our children. We need to be available in order for them to talk to us about their day at school, and how they are doing in general. We must be as available as a good customer service representative who is always ready to guide us through the aisle of a store to find what we need.

It is evident that we must work, but when we are home or on vacation with our children, we must make them feel loved and special. If they cannot talk to us because we are not around, they will talk to their friends, and potentially people who do not have their best interests at heart. If we do not take the time to teach them how to dress, they will learn it from watching music videos, on YouTube, or from their friends. Our kids need us to teach and train them so that they may have a pleasant experience in the world.

It matters what they wear; we do not want to attract the wrong attention to them before the right time. We must teach them to eat healthy and to take care of their body so that they enjoy a wholesome life. When we are available to do these things for our children, we have embraced our life as parents who want to help their children live well and to be happy.

Money is not always the answer to everything. In fact, in many instances, time is more valuable and important than money. Therefore, I encourage you parents to spend more active time with your children. Being in the same room with your children and sitting on the same couch with them does not mean that you are spending time together. The moments you share with your children should be meaningful; it should be time well spent doing something to create pleasant memories.

I once heard someone say that we are nothing but our memories. If that is true, we parents should strive to create wonderful memories with our children. Unfortunately, I cannot prescribe what one must do to create wonderful memories with children, but whatever you do to create wonderful memories, your children will greatly benefit and will be grateful to you for meeting their emotional, physical, educational, and financial needs. That is what I call embracing life as a parent.

Chapter 7
Embrace Your Children Equally

Joseph's father may have made a lot of mistakes in his life, but at least he was seriously involved in his children's lives. In fact, we can read it in Genesis 37 where Jacob displayed special love and care for his children. In verse 2, we are told about Jacob's family dynamics. The first thing we learned is that Jacob loved his children, but he loved Joseph, who was the son of his favorite wife, Rachel, more than his other children. Here is a man who loved all his children, but decided that he would love one more than the others.

Obviously, Jacob was following in the footsteps of his father, Isaac, who loved his brother Esau more than he loved him. One would think that Jacob would have learned from his rocky relationship with his brother, and not repeat the favoritism that his parents practiced. Jacob should have thought about his children's future and the way that they would live after his death. Regardless of Jacob's reason for loving Joseph more, it should have been intentionally kept secret. The brotherly love and affection between the siblings depended on the equal love of their parents.

The Bible says that Jacob loved Joseph more because he was the son of his old age. It does not matter why Jacob loved Joseph more than the other children. As parents, we must be careful not to show favoritism in the family, because it can disrupt the family harmony. Part of embracing life no matter the circumstances is to be fair with your children no matter their ages, aspirations in life, dispositions, and temperaments. We must accept our children as God has given them to us, and not penalize them for things that are beyond their control.

Joseph's brothers had nothing to do with Joseph's mother being barren for a while. They did not have a vote in the way and the time they were born. They did not choose their name, their voice, fingerprint, or their cognitive and intuitive abilities. Therefore, we must strive to treat our children equally, with fairness and love.

For instance, you might have a child who hates school, church, or anything that you think might be a good tool to help raise that child. You must find a way to embrace that child no matter what, by patiently trying your best to parent and be available as much as possible. It makes no sense to favor one child over the other because he or she resembles you, has your skin tone, your nose, your eyes, or your smile. It is not fair to the least favored child or children who had no control over their looks, temperament, and the mother from whose womb they were birthed.

Jacob is not a good role model when it comes to having favorites among his children. I encourage you parents to embrace all your children, and to attempt your best at not having, nor revealing, such divisive information.

We are told that Joseph was already a teenager, precisely 17 years of age, when his father was still spoiling him. Jacob probably gave Joseph special treatment around the house. He probably allowed Joseph to get away with things with which the other siblings could not. Jacob went so far as to making a special coat for his favorite son. He did the exact same thing that his mother did when he stole his brother's birthright. The older brothers' family inheritance was threatened by the special love bestowed on Joseph, who was the second to the last son. The other children hated Joseph just because they realized that their father loved them less.

I believe that children, even when they are not given a reason to think that they are loved less among their siblings, still secretly wonder if they are mommy's or daddy's favorite. We must intentionally work at convincing and proving to them that we have no favorites. It is critical that parents are equally involved in the life of their children to ensure that they have what they need as individuals. They are all unique in their perspectives and behaviors, and we must treat them as individuals who deserve our undivided attention.

Can you imagine being hated by your own brothers, sisters, or even parents? Can you imagine your own siblings talking about you? Are you someone who has despised your childhood because you were not your parents' favorite? Are you still struggling in your relationship with your siblings?

My little sister Rodeline and I used to fight over everything when we were growing up in Haiti. We argued frequently, chased each other around the house, and we held grudges against each other. One day we had a physical fight, and she hit me where every girl learned to hit a boy for a quick and complete submission. I fell on the ground in agony, but after I regained my strength, I chased her to get my childish revenge. She went and hid behind the outside kitchen door. I kicked the door, which hit her in the face and she started bleeding. I hated myself for hurting my little sister, who was two years younger than me. I spent the next 15 years apologizing to her, because the cut on her face left an ugly scar right above her lip. It was a reminder to me that I was a horrible big brother.

I wonder if Joseph's older brothers felt the guilt that I felt for my sister. She forgave me even if I did not forgive myself. We did not really like fighting and holding grudges, because it tainted the already somber atmosphere that we had at home with our father being gone and our mother being ill. Consequently, we let go of our grudges, we learned to not antagonize one another, and to be cool siblings again.

Now, as adult siblings, we no longer fight, and we still remember when to stop pushing each other's buttons. We have experienced hating one another as siblings, but it was not because we were lacking our parents' love. We did not fight because of favoritism in the home. However, I secretly felt that I was my mother's favorite child, simply because I was the only boy she had, but not because she confirmed that I was her favorite. I think that Jacob and his parents should not have openly had favorite children. I am happy that Jacob loved all his children and took care of them even though Joseph was his favorite.

I personally knew a young woman who was a senior at Oakwood University when I was a first-year student there. I did not know that she was going through so much family drama at the time. She looked very pretty and very peaceful. In fact, I almost asked her out. Unfortunately, I found out 10 years later that her own mother had kicked her out prior to her admission at Oakwood. She was still a little girl, but for no apparent valid reason, she was homeless while her mother had a comfortable abode. She knew that she was not her mother's favorite and that she was not loved by her mother. She was homeless, but God found a good Samaritan woman who embraced her no matter her circumstances.

She ended up at Oakwood University because a good Haitian woman adopted her. She traveled to Spain to learn Spanish, and later became a mother herself. I was told that she, unfortunately, had some complications delivering her baby, because her mother used witchcraft to hurt her and the baby. I find it hard to believe that a mother would try to use magic against her own baby girl, and had no remorse or shame about her actions.

That mother damaged her child in ways that she will never understand. Her hatred for her own daughter will affect her granddaughter's life, who had nothing to do with the cause of their feud. I cannot imagine how difficult it must have been for that young woman to love her siblings.

This mother's wicked actions against her daughter will have a ripple effect on the society at large. It might be hard for the little girl to have a "functional" family of her own. How can she ever trust the love of anyone else when she considers the way her own mother treated her? She may have trust issues. She may become paranoid, thinking that no one loves her, and that everyone is out to hurt her. The list of things that can happen to her because of her mother's treatment is inexhaustible. In fact, a year or two after her baby was born, she and the Haitian woman who took her in had a huge disagreement. She eventually moved out of the woman's house. I do not know the cause of their disagreement, but I knew that it was going to be hard for her to trust her adoptive parent.

I have not seen her in years. I am not sure how she and her daughter are doing. I can only hope that she truly embraced her life despite the way her mother treated her. It will be beneficial to her daughter, and it will give her daughter a chance to have a better childhood than what she unfortunately had.

Although the young woman in this story was not hated by her siblings, and Joseph's father did not hate him in the biblical story, we can see how each story both contrasts and relates to the other.

In the biblical story, Joseph was hated because of his father's outward expression of love toward him. I find it to be somewhat of an oxymoron. It is strange that he was hated simply because he was loved. It is like saying that he was rich because he was poor, or his horrible childhood was a recipe for a successful adulthood in Egypt. As oxymoronic as it seems, our experiences in life will always have a double meaning, whether we know it or not. I found this to be true in my own experience in Haiti.

For instance, I did not know how rich I was growing up in Haiti. Can one really be rich in Haiti? After all, many people love to promulgate that it is the poorest country in the western hemisphere, as if they did not contribute to its poverty. I was rich, but somehow, I felt as though I was poor.

Not having a refrigerator, a stove, a microwave, and an air conditioning unit made me feel dirt poor. My parents did not have a car in Haiti, therefore, we either took the city bus to work and school, or we walked everywhere. I drank lots of water at room temperature because my parents did not have a refrigerator. We cooked all our food from a fresh supply, and never had frozen food to unthaw. I did not drink too much juice unless it was made from squeezed lemon, orange, or grapefruit. I thought that I was poor because Haiti did not have the convenience of 24-hour electricity that most developed countries have. Consequently, I slept early at night, for I could not watch television.

I could not wait to come to the United States to have access to 24-hour electricity, a refrigerator, a stove, a microwave, running water, and a car. I thought that my standard of living was horrible, but having lived in the United States for twenty years, I have learned that I was rich in Haiti when I did not have electricity. I could sleep and enjoy a night of rest without allowing a television screen to hypnotize me. I was rich because I did not have a microwave to warm up my food. Studies have shown the health risks that come with having a microwave. I was rich when I did not have a refrigerator, because cold and frozen water is not good for the digestive system; it shrinks the blood vessels and forces the body to use extra energy to warm up the substance in preparation for digestion. I was rich in Haiti because I was poor when I lacked the hazardous household appliances.

In Haiti, I walked most of the time, and therefore I remained healthy. I did not have any knee problems, but now all of that has changed. I live in a "rich country" where I do not have to walk that much. I thought I was poor for not having a vehicle, but I found out it was a benefit to my health. I was rich in Haiti when I did not have a telephone to pollute my body with dangerous radiofrequencies that can cause cancer. Sadly, I thought that I was poor. A bad situation can always be seen as a good situation depending on the perspective.

Jacob's special love and affection for Joseph placed him in a terrible situation with his siblings and with the rest of his acquaintances. The poor child was lonely in a house full of siblings. Jacob had twelve sons. They talked about Joseph and whispered when he came around. I wonder how Joseph felt living in a home where his older siblings envied, and even hated him. As a child, it was not enough that his father loved him. As a matter of fact, his mother had passed away while he was still young. Joseph could have succumbed to the childhood pressure that weighed heavy on him. He could have changed his personality to persuade his brothers to love and accept him.

I was encouraged to know that Joseph did not change his character; he did not become rude to his father so that his siblings would love him. It is implied that Joseph embraced his life and became what his Creator intended for him to become. After all, he was destined to provide for the same people who caused him to experience both love and hate. Joseph was born into a family that had been dysfunctional for centuries. The notion of love in the home of Jacob was a contradiction with which the family had to live.

Being loved should be a great thing, but it often comes with the envy and jealousy of onlookers who might be a little insecure. They might not feel as loved, therefore they respond with hate. It is great to have the favor of a boss at work, and it is encouraging to feel appreciated, but do not ever forget that love attracts a little bit of envy from others. Do not be naive to think that everyone loves you and has your best interest at heart.

At one point, Joseph's brothers tore his special coat that his father made for him. At another, they attempted to murder their own little brother. They first put him in a pit to die alone, then they decided to sell their defenseless, scared, shivering, weeping, and vulnerable blood relative into slavery. They exposed him to hard labor, rape, torture, and imprisonment at the hands of complete blood thirsty, money hungry savages. Jacob's sons did to their little brother Joseph what some of the African rulers did to their African brothers back in the 1400s; they mercilessly sold their own kind to complete strangers, and did not think twice about their actions. It is what I call the "Judas Effect." Delivering a family member or a friend to cruel and heartless enemies is what Judas, the disciple, did to Jesus the Messiah.

I honestly do not think that a pack of wolves would surrender one of their own to a pack of lions. I have even seen on the animal planet herds of elephants defending their little ones against other carnivorous predators. If the animals whom we've said are devoid of reason know not to betray one another, if they somehow understand that they should protect one another and work in communities for their own survival, why do we who are "civilized" animals have no problem trading our own kind as a currency?

I have often wondered why the African rulers who sold some of their brothers to European and Arabian evil explorers did not go back to rescue them. I wondered the same thing about the brothers of Joseph. Why did they not attempt to return the money and rescue their little brother? They must have felt some type of remorse. One of them must have cried and carried the guilt. At least Judas tried to return the money for which he sold Jesus. He was not successful, but he seemed to be plagued with remorse.

I read the story of Jacob and Joseph several times. I have not yet found where Joseph's brothers expressed their guilt or acted remorseful. It was not until they were vulnerably brought to Egypt, and they had to face their little brother who had become as powerful as Pharaoh, that they became repentant and started to remorsefully lament.

Joseph followed in his father's and grandmother's footsteps when he tricked his brothers by hiding his favorite cup in their sac. His brothers were embarrassed and thought that God was punishing them for what they had done to their younger brother earlier in their life. They did not know where the cup came from and why it was hidden among their belongings. Joseph deceived them just as they'd deceived their father, who was deceived by his uncle Laban, who himself had deceived his father Isaac.

The older brothers were now deceived by their young brother whom they did not recognize. He was their younger brother, and he was probably proud to have so many older brothers from whom he thought protection was guaranteed. He was vulnerable and naive when they seized him. Why did they allow hate and envy to blind them to the point where they were willing to kill him?

Can you imagine the look of despair on the face of the young Joseph being put in chains; being loaded as merchandise for the profit of complete strangers? Can you imagine the millions of negative thoughts that plagued the mind of this little brother? The blind trust that he placed in his brothers, the patience he had with their indifferences, and the many times he probably covered for their mistakes? As far as the young Joseph was concerned, his life was over when the brothers put him in the pit. It was over when they tore his clothes; he was probably carried away half-naked. He must have thought his life was over when his brothers turned their backs on him. Imagine with me, if you will, the young Joseph in a new land, embracing his life and his new circumstances. Can you see the many days and nights that he wept, and no family members were available to console him? Can you see him deal with the rejection of his brothers, the loss of his family, and the love that caused him to become a slave? Can you see him learning to cope with his new life as a child?

He was accused of rape, wrongfully imprisoned, forgotten among criminals for a while, until the time when his Creator ushered him into his purpose and his destiny to save his father and siblings from the imminent starvation that were to come on them.

I continue to see parallels in Joseph's story with the story of my ancestors who were unloaded as cargo on the shores of Hispaniola. It makes me reflect on the state of their children, and the way they were treated. What an awful childhood they had; the horror they had experienced seeing their parents whipped, raped, and tortured; being sold away to other evil slave owners to purposely destroy their family; the nightmare of being sold to strangers and becoming their property forever.

Away from the love and comfort of their family, slave children around the world must have cried and wept like Joseph. There were even stories of evil slave owners who raped fathers in front of their children and the entire community to break any spirit of rebellion.

Fortunately for Joseph, the Bible says that God was with him, and that God prospered him in everything that he did. I am sure that Joseph cried, but after the tears, he embraced his life, and God was with him in his captors' foreign land.

He certainly had some difficult moments. His family members were too far away to help him, but God did not abandon him. He was ordering his steps and He was working behind the scenes to ensure that Joseph was successful. Similarly, the children of African slaves around the world embraced their life. They had and continue to have, even in the 21st century, difficult moments in the world. Some of them continue to suffer from hunger, diseases, neglect, lynching, and other kinds of injustices. But God has not abandoned them. Or should I say us?

The Lord is ordering their steps and He is working behind the scenes to bring them success in their life in the new world. Soon they will say to their oppressors, "I do not hate you for violating my basic human rights. I do not hate you for keeping financial resources from me and making fun of my poverty. I do not hate you for robbing me of my spirituality, dignity, and sanity. I do not hate you, because what you meant for evil, the Creator meant it for good for a greater purpose; one that will serve to rescue humanity from the plague of racism and endless violence.

When we embrace our life no matter what our childhood may have been, we eventually realize our purpose and calling. Jacob thought that his beloved son was dead. He became suicidal and neglected his other children. As parents today, we should be careful to not stop living if something bad happens to one of our children. We must continue to live and take care of the remaining precious children who need us and believe in us.

As much as possible, we must strive to make the lives of children enjoyable, and help them create great childhood memories. We must remember that they did not ask to be born, and that we must help them reach their full potential. We might be raising the next queens, kings, presidents, doctors, healers, or scientists. We may never know who we are raising, and for what purpose they were born.

Sometimes children might frustrate us. They might make our days painful and stressful, but we should remember that we did the same thing to our parents.

One time, my wife called me and told me that Robyn does not make her days easy; sometimes our little princess fights us even to change her diapers. Even in that small matter, we as her parents should embrace our life. We should embrace the little struggle that our daughter puts up every time we try to bathe her. We should embrace our life every time she fights us, even when we try to feed her. We should embrace our life when she fights us as we try to put her clothes on. We do not know what the Lord has purposed her to become. We have no idea whose life she is going to change, therefore, we must be patient with our little girl, and strive to give her the best childhood that she can ever have. We promise to love her and cherish her, so that when her time comes, she will do the same for others and her own family.

If Jacob knew that Joseph was destined to save his tribe from imminent starvation, he would have probably not lost hope when his sons lied and said that Joseph was murdered. If Joseph's siblings knew that he was predestined to be a leader in Egypt—a man of power in a foreign land—they would have probably not attempted to sell him to slave traders, let alone try to murder him.

I am almost certain that people would treat children better

if they could see their future and purpose. We all would be treated differently if our life purpose was made public from childhood. I believe that even we would treat ourselves better if we knew for a fact the mission of our existence. Since most of us are ignorant of our calling, we must embrace our life in preparation for that which lays ahead. The next generation's survival depends on our acceptance of our current life situation and past experiences.

Josephs brothers did not recognize their little brother. He was no longer the clumsy little brother who could not defend himself. He had become a mighty man of valor who was loved and respected by the Egyptians. He was the second in command in Egypt, and thus controlled the surrounding villages around his dominion. God had prepared a table before Joseph and his older brothers. He was so blessed that his former envious brothers could not even imagine it.

Joseph had the power in his hand to make his brothers pay for what they had done to him. He could have put them in prison for years. He could have thrown them in solitary confinement for years, or he could have called some slave traders and sold his older brothers into slavery in retaliation for their evil past actions. But instead, Joseph settled on tricking them by putting his favorite cup in one of their sacs of grains.

The brothers had left their father's home and travelled to Egypt to buy food during a prolonged famine. Joseph recognized them, but they did not recognize him. People who hurt us in the past—those who bullied us at school and at the bus stop, the hypocrite friends who spread rumors about us on social media, and neighbors who made fun of us—have a tendency of catching amnesia when God blesses us. When we become mighty, we still remember the people who wronged us. Most of the time, we do not remember those who were a blessing in our life, but we tend to never let go of those who hurt us the most. We remember, but they do not.

My wife told me a sad story about her middle school years

at a public school. She said that she was walking in the halls of the school when one of the school's female bullies thrusted her. The bully was an obese and insecure little girl who wanted attention. She pushed my wife from the back with all her might. My poor, introvert wife fell to the ground and was embarrassed. I do not blame the little bully for what she did to my wife, because she might have had a personal reason why she bullied her classmates. She might have had a horrible life at home, and she was probably deprived of responsible and available parents to raise her.

I blamed the school and her parents for her actions. I am not saying that she was completely innocent. Some schools intentionally work at ensuring that bullying does not occur, and that every child has a civil learning environment.

I started working for a school in 2015, and I still work there as I type this paragraph on the 25th of September 2017. I have not seen any bullying that involved pushing and shoving. Bullies do not usually remember the faces or names of the people they have hurt. That is why Joseph's brothers did not recognize him in Egypt.

They did not recognize Joseph, because his outward appearance was different than that which they knew him to look like physically. The last time they'd seen him, he was weak and vulnerable. He needed their help and he needed their affirmation. Their feeble previous memory of him was that of a pitiful and dying prey who was at the mercy of his predator. They could not imagine that their little brother, whom they sold to strangers, condemned to live as a slave, could rise and assume such a position of power in a foreign land.

I can imagine the brothers of Joseph, with bewildered faces, troubled hearts, trembling knees, jaws dropped, and their soul wishing to leave their body, seeking a peaceful place to rest. They must have argued among themselves. They might have given themselves several different reasons why the powerful man whose serene face they were beholding could not be their little brother.

I FEEL LIKE PREACHING NOW!

They sent him away empty-handed. They sent him away a homeless child. They sent him away bound as a slave whose duty was to follow orders. He was probably sent away hungry with dried lips, ashy arms, and ashy legs. He was probably sent away confused and clumsy. He was probably sent away upset. But now, they were looking at a rich man. They were in the presence of a well-respected leader. They were fearfully admiring a man who could sleep in all the castles, pyramids, and hotels of Egypt.

They felt vulnerable sitting in the presence of their once feeble and powerless little brother who could eat at all the restaurants of Egypt; whose net worth was second to that of the pharaoh. They must have felt remorseful. Their once powerless little brother had become a powerful and mighty ruler, who at the snap of his fingers could send them away for a long and sudden nightmare of a life.

Was Joseph planning to take revenge on them? Was he holding grudges that were going to be the demise of his wicked older brothers?

Everything that happened to Joseph through the crooked hearts of his older brothers were used by God to make him the leader that he saw in his dreams when he was yet a little child. Joseph understood that the power he had over his older wicked brothers, as well as his leadership position, was awarded by the Lord through Pharaoh. Joseph knew in his heart that if it had not been for the Lord who was with him when he was being shipped to Egypt as a slave—he knew in his heart that if it had not been for the Lord who was with him when he wept, and when he was plunged deep as a submarine in the vast ocean of loneliness--he would not have become so powerful in a foreign land.

Joseph knew that his social status was rooted in his destiny. He knew that the Lord was the reason for his success. While his brothers were secretly asking one another what would become of them; while they were secretly planning their escape; while they were finally accepting their fate, and were deciding to confess that their actions were evil and heartless; and while they began to weep and to beg that their little brother would not seek revenge on them after the death of their elderly father, the Bible said that Joseph rose from his lofty position of power and ordered his Egyptian secret service agents, his department of homeland security, and his FBI agents to leave the room and not return regardless of any commotion that they might hear from the outside.

Joseph wanted to see all his brothers, and he wanted to see his beloved father. He deceived the few brothers who came, and bribed them to bring their father and the rest of their family to Egypt. They did not know who he was, and consequently, they were fearful for their life.

People who hurt you will become fearful of you once they realize who you are and when God raises you up. They will become paranoid thinking that you will treat them as badly as they treated you.

Joseph cried so loud that the Egyptians heard him. His cry and his tears were indicative of the depth of his pain. We know that he was hurt and that he was experiencing mixed emotions based on the following question that he asked: "Is my father still living?"

He cried because he missed his father. He cried because he had not seen him in a long time. He cried because he did not know if he was still alive. He cried because his brothers did not recognize him. When you know your purpose in life—when you have embraced your life—you do not allow your social power to take away your ability to both empathize and sympathize. Joseph saw that his brothers were terrified, and he knew that they were being hard on themselves. Their faces were guilt ridden; they did not look good at all.

He had previously overheard them speaking about their guilt in their own language. They did not know that he understood what they were saying. Joseph's mind was more elevated than theirs. He knew what was going to happen, and that the Lord had chosen him to save them. His brothers did not know that he had embraced his life, and that he had accepted his purpose. They did not know that through many years of suffering, their little brother had acquired a wealth of knowledge and a depth of understanding that was beyond their grasp.

He said, "I am Joseph." Then he said, "Come close to me."

His knowledge of his purpose did not allow him to consciously afflict pain on those who had hurt him in the past. The intentional embracement of his life through his experience with people and God helped him to become their benefactor. They expected him to be as mean to them as they had been when he was vulnerable. They were bracing themselves to receive what they rightfully deserved. They expected to be severely punished, but their little brother invited them to come closer. People who have hurt you in the past will have unsurmountable mountains of difficulty accepting your genuine love.

I would be afraid if I knew that I'd hurt someone bad in the past who now had power over my life. Seeing them in the position of power would automatically strike fear in my being. I would be terrified to be in the same room with them, let alone for that same person to invite me to come closer. The precarious predicament of the older brothers vis-à-vis their powerful younger brother Joseph makes me reflect on the way black and white people treat each other in the world.

Although the brothers were terrified, Joseph was both sad and happy that they were finally going to be a family again. When you embrace your life, you look for opportunities to reunite with those who hurt you. When you embrace your life, you do not use your power to crush your enemies, rather you bring them closer to you, and you shower them with good things. Joseph told his brothers to bring their father and all their belongings to Egypt. He wanted to provide a place for them to live, a place where they would have food to eat, and where the famine would not affect them. Joseph said, "I will provide for you." What a peaceful world our children would have if all nations of the world provided for each other.

Would you provide for somebody who broke your heart in the past? Would you provide for someone who embarrassed you in middle or high school? Would you provide for siblings who were not around when you needed them the most? Would you provide for somebody who hurt you that bad in the past? Would you provide for a mother who abandoned you when you needed her the most? Would you provide for a father who molested you when you were most vulnerable? Would you provide for those who cost you so much pain, loneliness, and money? Would you provide for a spouse who left you in your most vulnerable moments? Would you provide for a disrespectful child who ran away from home? Would you provide for someone who mutilated your body, shot your sons in the streets like animals, and destabilize your country intentionally?

Well, I have the honor to announce to you that when you truly embrace your life, you will provide for those who hurt you the most. Like Joseph, you will know that God placed you in a position of power to serve and meet someone else's needs. When you reflect on the goodness of the Lord and the way He has provided for you, it becomes easier to provide for those who were the cause of your tears. You become a Joseph when you are in a position to hire, fire, feed, arrest, donate, teach, defend, rescue, and care for people who wronged you in the past. Embracing your life in that situation is to say with Joseph, "What you meant for evil, the Lord used it for my benefit."

Chapter 8
Politics Create Dysfunctional Homes

There is another group of children who suffer daily in America, and certainly around the world. Sometimes they are not physically abused, but they are psychologically debilitated. They are emotionally injured because they mourn the loss of a parent because of unjust, race-motivated police or civilian shootings, false arrest, or wrongful convictions that are still rampant throughout the world, especially in the United States of America.

Reading Twitter tweets, Facebook posts, and hearing insensitive comments about the victims after their unfortunate and unjustified murder makes it hard for the poor surviving children to move on with their shattered life. They become forgotten, and they are avoided at all cost, because it is hard for people to help them deal with the unbearable pain inflicted on them.

In August 2017, one of my friends mourned the loss of his uncle back in Haiti. His uncle was murdered by Haitian police, apparently for no obvious reasons. He allegedly left home one sunny morning, and was caught in a crossfire during a public demonstration in Port-au-Prince. He died, leaving young children behind who will most likely grow up orphans in need of food, shelter, and clothing. Whether the officers shot my friend's uncle in self-defense, or they did it by mistake, their action left a bottomless void in those children's lives. Given that Haiti is still a country without a solid judicial system, the officers will probably not be prosecuted.

Unfortunately, the orphans must figure life out alone, or be dependent on the mercies of good Samaritans. In any case, they will need to embrace their new life and live out their purpose. The Creator must have made those children for a reason. At some point in their predictable hard life, He will reveal it to them. Haiti needs a new generation of children who will move it into new political arenas. Perhaps one of the million orphans will be a messiah to the Haitian people. A messiah who will not preach religious dogma, but one who will feed the hungry, clothe the naked, provide shelter for the homeless, and visit the incarcerated. It is certainly time for this long-awaited messiah to come and preach liberation and not judgment.

There are many other similar cases throughout the world, and especially in the United States. One out of many depressing police tragedies brings pain to my soul. It is one that leaves me weak and hopeless when I reflect on the state of mind of the four-year-old girl who witnessed it. My heart hurts when I think of a toddler in the state of Louisiana who was in a vehicle with her mother, and accompanied by her mother's male friend. The little girl witnessed the gruesome murder of someone she knew and loved. A police officer shot a bullet in the vehicle only a few feet away from the little girl. Can you imagine her trauma? What if it were you or your lovely four-year-old?

I try not to think about her and what she went through, but her story stayed on my mind. I imagine that it must have been hard enough for the child to see a gun pointed at someone she loved. I am sure the release of the bullet through a loud bang was enough to make her soul jump out of her body, or even worse, to see life slowly leaving out of someone she loved.

Children do not understand why their father, mother, or friends are shot by police officers who are sworn to protect them. Those children are given a bad hand in life with which they must deal. If no one teaches them to embrace that which was given them, and learn to find a purpose in it, those children might be doomed to become vindictive, suicidal, or simply evil. They might become a terror to themselves and to the rest of us.

I constantly reflect on the grief and anger the children who lost their parents in the World Trade Center feel. Some children had no idea that September 11, 2001 was the last day they had on earth with their mother, father, uncle or aunt. There were people, motivated by revenge and hate, who came to take the life of a parent who had children at home. Their young minds will find a way to cope with everything, but we as adults must find a way to help them embrace their new life and make the best of it. Children all around the world suffer from both domestic and foreign terror attacks. They are too young to comprehend the reason for their loss. Not helping them is to allow a vindictive spirit to transform them into monsters who will keep the cycle of violence alive.

I know from experience the fear that grips the heart of children growing up in war zones. As a child in Haiti, at night there were times when my mother would hide us under a bed for fear that we would be hit by a stray bullet. Our little hearts used to beat faster than normal, and we wanted the night to be over so that daylight could rescue us from the thugs and their guns. The site of an actual gun would have killed us. If a man in a police uniform was standing a few feet away from us with a gun pointed in our direction, my siblings and I would have urinated on ourselves.

I cannot begin to imagine the life of that little girl in Louisiana after the murder she witnessed. Was there any purpose to what this little girl experienced? I dare to say yes. As horrible and heartless as it sounds, there is always a purpose to our childhood experiences. We may not know it at the time, but there is a purpose to them. I believe that the Lord will give the girl the strength that she will need to embrace her life despite of what she endured as a toddler. God might be preparing her to become the solution to unjust police murdering in America. She might be destined to be a lawmaker or a judge. She is certainly not aware of her calling in life, but her Maker and Creator knows exactly why she was born.

Like Jesus, one day she might be able to say, "For this reason I was born," or "For that reason came I into the world." Other children around the world will one day find their life purpose, and will become the solution to the problems inherited from past wicked generations.

I sincerely believe that one of the children we see on television, at church, at the grocery store, in our neighborhood, or in our classrooms, is destined to make life better for the rest of us. For this reason, we must allow and teach them to embrace the life and childhood that destiny gave them, no matter how unfair their circumstances, and regardless of how painful their experience. It will usher them right into their purpose. As in the story of Joseph, his siblings were not the chosen ones to bring the rest of their family and neighbors out of the imminent famine that was upon them. Joseph was born into a situation where both his parents were unable to help him. He had to figure it out alone. His Creator guided him through the process, but it was *his* journey, not that of his brothers.

Whether we like it or not, our precious children have a work to do in the world. They will invent the next great piece of equipment or technological device that will enable us to live longer, healthier, to be safer, and to live stress-free. One of them will come up with the million-dollar idea that will revolutionize race relations across the globe. The next Moses, Lao-tzu, Buddha, Confucius, Jesus Christ, Muhammad, Gandhi, Martin Luther King, or Malcom X could be one of the toddlers that you have at home.

The next Sojourner Truth (who was an African American Abolitionist and Women's Rights Activist), the next Mother Theresa (who was an Albanian nun and charity worker), and the next Rosa Parks (who refused to give up her seat to racist people in Montgomery, Alabama) might be in your daycare playing with other children who will, one day, benefit from their accomplishments. You may be changing the diaper of a little girl or a little boy who might be deified for his or her accomplishments later in life.

Embracing my life means to make the best out of what I have now, while striving for better. It means that I must treat others with dignity and respect, because I do not know anything about their future. They might be the angel that the Lord decides to use for my deliverance. The interesting thing about life is that our siblings, classmates, neighbors, colleagues, or even students, may have been commissioned to bless us, help us, teach us, sit by us when no one else would for social reasons, or even save our life at some point in our conscious existence.

Life is hard for all of us at different levels, but not all of us decide to embrace our life on our own respective levels of challenges. Being part of the same human family bids us to seek out our purpose and fulfil our destiny. We each have a role to play as a family member. Fortunately, or unfortunately, the Creator has embedded it in our DNA, and strategically caused us to be born in the geographical location of the world that needs us the most.

There is no reason to go about life depressed and suicidal when one knows that everything serves a greater purpose. We may not understand our life challenges, or we may not like them, but your maker knows and understands it all.

In the policies that we make, we need to think about our children and keep them in the forefront of all our decision-making in government. Let us embrace our life and act like Joseph, who worked directly under Pharaoh to make policies and help create a better life for those living in Egypt. Joseph was a God-fearing man who ran away from Potiphar's wife when she attempted to seduce him. I know that he feared the Lord, because he said to the woman that he would not sin against God and betray the trust of Potiphar, his employer, who happened to be her husband.

What a perfect world our children would have if all the government workers were men of principles who feared a righteous God. The same way the Lord had purposed Joseph to become a government agent in Egypt, I believe that He has many of His agents currently working for the police department, the fire station, and Congress. Some are working in federal buildings, in the prisons, and in the jails. The Lord has many Josephs who are working at all levels of government. We should be able to find them at both the federal and the state level.

Many people were born to serve the rest of us as government agents. Several were born to lead the rest of us. They were born to protect the defenseless. They came to life to heal the rest of us. They became conscious to edify our souls, and still others were born to teach and educate our children. The story of Joseph demonstrates that we were all born to meet a need, and ultimately serve a purpose.

For those of us who were born to be a Joseph at Potiphar's house, let us be righteous and work as if we were hired by God. If we work for the government with a mindset of not sinning against God, if we work with the mindset of practicing righteousness, being good to those and for those we work, we will create a better world for our children. We should work to save lives and work to prevent chaos. Our work should be to make the life of children an enjoyable childhood. Let us embrace our life at every level of our society. Let us use our professions to minister and to serve the greater need of our community.

Police officers, let us serve our purpose by becoming the hands of God on earth to protect and not to cause pain unjustly. Judges, let us become the mouthpiece of the Creator from whose lips everyone can expect fair and equal justice. Lawyers, let us become ministers of God on earth who defend the cases of the poor as well as the cases of the rich. Lawmakers, let us work to create laws that make planet earth a haven for children to explore, and for their parents to raise them without fear. Let us all embrace our life and turn our profession or our job into a ministry that saves and improves life.

If we look at our job as a ministry, which the sole purpose is to meet the needs of others, we are guaranteed to make someone's life a little better, even if it is just for one day, one hour, or one minute. Let us all act as ministers and save the life of many children and adults who are on the verge of dying. Let us all play an active role in making social justice a reality.

If the terminology "minister of God" does not sit well with you, or the idea of working for a "fictional" God sounds too primitive, allow me to invite you to think of yourself as a benevolent god who diligently looks for souls to bless. Just entertain the idea for a moment. What if you acted as a benevolent god toward the rest of us? Or better yet, what if we all acted as benevolent gods who continuously seek opportunities to outdo one another by promptly ministering to the needs of people? I am convinced that the millions of orphans, as well as the thousands of children who are growing up in single-parent homes, would be blessed to have the rest of us "gods" competing to shower on them our blessings. In fact, I am persuaded that each one of us would love to have a benevolent God who provides for our every need.

I want to invite those who have the gift of music to think about the suffering children of the world. Musicians, let us embrace our life and create music that heals, music that empowers, music that transcends the soul, and music that brings peace to the mind. Every talent and gift is given to serve others.

Rappers, let us create beats and lyrics that uplift our listeners, and educate and inform our young people. Rock stars, let us create music that discourages the use of drugs, and encourages our fans to uplift the children and save our world. We should use our position of leadership to create and to inspire our audience to embrace their life and serve their purpose. Our music should teach young children to act as the heroes and role models of their communities. Let us use our talents to persuade our fans to embrace their life, and to go out into the world to find some needs that must be met.

I have seen many inspirational movies that make me cry like a baby. I never cry when a villain kills or tortures his or her victims; I simply do not watch the gruesome murdering scenes. I only cry when evil characters had a change of heart and became good Samaritans who helped those around them. What if all the movies that we produced were aimed at inspiring a safer and better world for our children?

Executives and investors, let us create businesses that are not solely aimed at generating major capitals, but let us use our business platforms to restore dignity in the mothers and fathers whom we employ. Our business ventures should put food on many tables, and provide a safe environment for our children to grow. Let us generate more money so that we may become a father to the fatherless, or a mother to the motherless.

Why do we not create businesses that give back to the community? Why do we not help struggling parents to create a memorable childhood for their children? We have created a mess in the world by exploiting its resources and ignoring each other's wellbeing. That is the reason we have so many orphans amongst us.

We have created an influx of prisoners to our jail system, because we do not actively and systematically work at meeting the population's needs. If we were actively working toward a wholesome and healthy population, we would have a mentally, financially, psychologically, intellectually, and socially healthy world.

Unfortunately, we do not have a healthy world. We manufacture hospital patients with our polluted waters and foods with which we feed our children. We create drug addicts so that they can continue to buy our products. We gentrify low-income communities, and create homeless families who do not have enough money to relocate, or people who do not have enough knowledge and resources. When it is all said and done, the children suffer the most.

Let us embrace our life and fix our problems by becoming ministers, or by becoming benevolent gods who persistently seek those in need, with the sole purpose to improve their life. The world is waiting for ministers of God. The hungry children are especially waiting for benevolent gods who will bring them food, shelter, and clothing; who will visit them in prison, and who will be there for them when they are bullied.

Children love the idea of Santa Clause, because it represents what we adults hope would happen in real life. We would love to have such a hero who would come down our chimney as a benevolent provider.

Every Christmas, those of us who participate in the tradition, voluntarily become Santa to bring joy to the faces of our children. What if we embrace our life and become a year-round Santa who provides not only for our biological children, but for children in general, especially the orphans? What if we become the God in whom we want our children to believe? Let us embrace our life and be the superhero, the superman, or the superwoman we wished was real. For the benefits of the children, **let us become Santa to make them happy, and not Satan to make them miserable**.

The reason why children love superhero movies or animations is because the superhero seems to always go after a well-known and hated villain. He is the cause of every pain, and he selfishly brings death and destruction to everyone. He poisons water supplies, he sets people and things on fire, and he domestically and internationally terrorizes all. He promotes genocide, he leaves hopeless children behind, and he destroys families and properties. Children naturally despise such a character, but they instinctively love the superhero who eventually defeats the dreaded villain. Children have a natural yearning for justice and fairness.

There are many villains in the world who are selfishly causing pain in their community as well as other people's community. When I reflect on the wickedness of the villains I see in the news daily, if I were not persuaded that some of us are going to assume our superhero position and make our children proud, I would be discouraged. We can all defeat our local villains by embracing our life and doing good in the community.

Let us work to bring joy and peace to the faces of children worldwide. Let us vow to not simply work for money and wealth, but to work to meet a need. I am embracing my life as a teacher. I want to teach the precious children who come to me for a linguistic experience. I vow to be kind to them and prepare them to go out into the world and meet a need. I want them to become a francophone superhero who can minister to both Anglophones and Francophones.

Let us embrace our life wherever we are geographically and emotionally. Let us embrace our life for the sake of the children. Let us do it for their children's children, and especially for the world's children who have been hurt by our politics. They are awaiting our arrival. Let us become the answer to their prayers. Let us dry their eyes and make them smile forever.

Pastors, if anyone should embrace life and turn a profession into a ministry to meet the needs of others, we should be the first ones to say, "Yes, Lord, I will." We were called to primarily meet the needs of our community by feeding the hungry, visiting the sick, visiting the incarcerated, providing shelters for those who have no homes, and clothe the naked. It is true that we were called to preach good news; the excellent news that the Messiah saves. By definition, the word Messiah means "anointed one."

In the Old Testament, prophets, priests, kings, and individuals who were selected for a special purpose were anointed with oil. They were anointed to meet a special need of the community. Therefore, they were all messiahs! Putting oil on their heads, and sometimes putting it on other parts of their body, gave them authority to minister to the rest of their society. The Messiah's job was and is to save lives. That is exactly what the prophets, the kings, and the priests used to do in the Old Testament.

Kings were anointed to protect their kingdoms, and priests were anointed to meet the spiritual and physical healing needs of their community. Judges were anointed to help keep peace in the community, and Levites were anointed to take care of the worship service. All of the above-mentioned messiahs were chosen to meet the need of their community. Therefore, the messiahs were saving lives by meeting the needs of their community. Once they were chosen to serve their community, they embraced their life.

For Christians who adhere to the Old Testament principles and reinterpret some of them to better serve the church, instead of anointing with oil individuals who would serve the community, they now ordain them. Being ordained, they can legally marry their parishioners, preach their doctrine, feed the hungry, clothe the naked, and ultimately make their parishioners' lives better by meeting their needs.

The good news for which they were ordained to preach is to give hope in times of hopelessness; to console the afflicted, to educate, to edify, to uplift, and to encourage their audience to live in righteousness.

Just as the Old Testament priests, Levites, judges, and kings embraced their life to meet the specific needs of their community, we, as ministers in the New Testament, should embrace our life and become messiahs for our church members. We need to become messiahs that save people from poverty and a life of debauchery. Let us save them from a life of crime. We can save their children's lives, and keep them from ending up in prison. Let us deliver them from drugs and prostitution. Let us make our pastoring job a true ministry, where the entire focus is not on earning money, but on helping people to improve their life here on earth.

We must embrace our life as ministers and create a safe environment for our parishioners' children to thrive. Our church should not only have weekly Bible studies that teach our church members about a distant heaven, it should not only teach them faithfulness in their tithes and offering, but it should also teach church members how to remain out of debt, how to practice group economics, and how to have and maintain healthy eating habits. We should teach them investments and savings principles from the Word. They need to know many more biblical and life principles from which they can benefit.

Let us embrace our life as ministers and start schools where our children can be educated, community centers where our children can have fun and stay away from trouble, and open safe and clean daycares where our little ones can be nurtured away from home. Let us start orphanages to provide a better life to the many children in and out of our community who have no parents.

Messiahs, let us save our parishioners financially by creating jobs for them. Let us use their tithes and offering money to create a community where they can work and earn a living. We can employ them in the barbershops that we create for them, and we can employ them in the restaurant that we create for them. We can employ them in our own grocery stores, banks, and clinics where our nurses and doctors can meet their health needs. We can employ them in our own daycares, orphanages, and church fitness centers, where both our youth and elderly members can come to work out and stay in shape.

We can have our own retirement homes where our parents and grandparents can live in a community designed to meet their needs. They can teach at our schools, and fix and maintain our cars at our own mechanic shops.

There are so many more opportunities that we can create for each other as we begin to meet each other's needs. We can employ our members as security officers in all those businesses. Keeping our money in our community ensures that the storehouse of Malachi chapter 3 verse 10 always has enough to take care of its members.

I know a Haitian proverb that says, "Grès kochon wan

kwit kochon an." It means that we can bake or cook our pork with its own grease. We will always have enough money to employ felons, enough to take care of the sick, enough to pay our members' bills, and enough to give free rent to those homeless living souls of our community, as well as other communities. The Messiah's job was to save, therefore, let us embrace our life as ministers and save our church members financially.

Let us embrace our life as anointed ones to save our members spiritually. We can save them spiritually by teaching them about their being and the ultimate Being who created them. If we teach them that they have been wonderfully constructed as a trinity, where their body is the shell of their soul, and their soul is the seat of their spirit, they will understand the necessity to take care of the body by eating healthy. They will understand how crucial it is to maintain the health of their soul by having positive experiences. They will appreciate a good worship service where songs, prayers, and meditation edifies their soul and feeds their spirit.

As ministers of God on behalf of our community, as messiahs who have been anointed to save our church members, we can teach them spiritually when we lift their minds above the mundane things of this world. Through us, God will provide for His children financial and spiritual needs. Let us not teach our members to be religious fanatics, rather let us teach them to be spiritual on their approach.

When I first moved to Birmingham, Alabama for a teaching job, Larry was one of my coworkers who invited me to his thriving church. He sang the praises of his young pastor who did not care about getting rich off his members' tithes and offerings, but rather cared about the welfare of his people. Mr. Larry would share with me all the things that he learned from the worship service. I know that he wanted me to visit his church, and one day I decided to visit.

When I arrived, there was a certain positive energy in and all around the vicinity of the church. I went to the 11 o'clock service and was blessed to experience a dynamic worship atmosphere where the praise team members, the musicians, the congregants, along with their pastor, were all spiritually synchronized. They seemed to have forgotten about their physical bodies, and successfully elevated their mind to the throne of their God.

It was so interactive that even the many guests, such as myself, were magnetically pulled and spiritually coerced to join in the worship experience. I was happy to have been a part of such an addictive worship service at New Rising Star Church. The sermon, which was preached by Pastor Thomas Beavers, the senior pastor of the church, added a higher dimension to the worship experience.

I was totally satisfied with the spiritual aspect of the church. When it was time for the announcements, I learned that the church was involved in many different ministries to take care of the needs of the community. The church had a program where every so often they invited employers from the community who had at least one job position open. The employers provided employment for their members. The church had a community center for their children, and they provided free groceries and a hot meal for those who attended Bible studies on Wednesdays.

During the Thanksgiving holiday, they gave free turkeys to the community. Throughout the year they gave free clothes and food to the community at large. They had a thriving daycare, and they were in the process of starting a charter school for the community.

They were interested in teaching the people financial literacy, and offered their members educational camps during the summer. They had uplifting programs for singles, as well as programs for married couples.

The pastor seemed to have plenty more on his mind to do for the members of his community. He acted like the young David who was on fire for the Lord and wanted to kill Goliath when the elders, soldiers, and experienced men were scared. I was hooked; I was awed to find a church that was attempting to do what the biblical church in the last days is supposed to do.

I am positive that there were probably other churches in the Birmingham area where the needs of the community were being met, but New Rising Star seemed to be one of the churches where the anointed ones were saving people's lives.

I saw many children at that church who seemed to be happy, and I also saw many adults who were proud to be part of that community. In fact, as we were leaving the church from our first visit, my wife said that it was great to see so many smiling faces enjoying the worship service.

I was happy with my visit to that Birmingham church, because I saw that the pastor was not a wolf in sheep's clothing who was exploiting his members. I saw that he was not interested in making them religious robots, but rather spiritual beings. I loved the fact that he truly cared and worked hard to minister to the members' body, soul, and spirit.

I thanked Mr. Larry for the invitation to his church, and I continued to go after that first time. It is our job as ministers to make sure that our church members prosper at all levels of their existence. Embracing our life as ministers is to become messiahs that save the community, and make children love the idea of having church. When they grow up to become adults, they will not ridicule their childhood experience in the church.

Chapter 9
Embracing Life Even in Prison

If you find yourself in prison while reading this book, and if you know that you are incarcerated wrongfully, or if you are reading this book and you have a sibling, parent, or a family member who you know has been wrongfully sentenced to prison, I want to use the story of Joseph to hopefully help you look forward to realizing that there is a purpose to life in general.

Joseph was born to be second to the pharaoh in Egypt, yet he found himself in prison and innocent. He was born to be a savior to not only his own people, but also to those who would mistreat, reject, and sell him as a slave. Even if he was born for the benefits of others, many people misguided by ignorance inflicted pain on him.

Joseph had a couple of dreams about his destiny, but I do not believe that he clearly knew what his purpose was. I am sure that he had no rational explanation for the way his brothers treated him, and the way Potiphar's wife accused him of sexual harassment. Joseph must have been devastated just reflecting on the false accusations against him, and the rejection from his family.

I imagine that it is one thing to lose your freedom because you are guilty and you are paying for your mistakes, but it is another thing to be behind bars because you were wrongfully convicted, or simply accused. Such is the plight of black and brown people in America.

Strategic systematic racism in the States created a platform to incarcerate minorities at a greater proportion than the dominant culture. Many of my brothers and sisters are imprisoned because poverty led them to criminal behaviors, or because they were in the company of the wrong group of people. Some were probably accused, like Joseph, and others were set up by those who were supposed to protect and serve them. Many evil and wicked people planted evidence or falsified their report to put them in prison, which left their children without a provider. When this happens, sometimes families are destroyed and children are placed in the care of a foster parent who is sometimes secretly abusive.

It is morally wrong to intentionally destroy people's lives by wrongfully placing them in an earthly hell. Justice demands that a criminal who has murdered his family or innocent people be punished, and at the same time, it condemns injustice.

I recently watched a prison documentary posted on YouTube by the National Geographic Channel. I learned a horrific story about a young man named Kenneth Young. He was 14 years old when he committed an attempted armed robbery, persuaded by a man who was 24 years old at the time. Although Kenneth was a child, the state of Florida sentenced him to four consecutive life in prison sentences for having committed a robbery with a gun. According to the documentary, the United States of America happened to be the only country in the world that sentenced children to die in prison. Even though Kenneth was only 14 years of age, the Florida justice system was ready to put him in prison for the rest of his life.

I praise the Lord for godly lawyers who still possess their humanity; some of them decided to start fighting the legal system and protested the sentencing of children to life in prison. They took their case before the Supreme Court. Their efforts were rewarded when in 2010, the US Supreme Court ruled that a juvenile life sentence is illegal for crimes that did not involve a murder.

My heart bled when I learned through the documentary that there were more than 2,000 inmates who were sentenced to life in prison while they were children. Florida had over 60 cases of children sentenced to death.

Kenneth Young grew up in a low-income housing project with his mother, who was a drug addict. Kenneth said that his mother used to lock him and his sister in the house all day, and half of the time they did not even know where she was or when she would come back home. He said that he used to get on his bike and ride around the neighborhood looking for his mother. He claimed that sometimes he would find his mother strung out somewhere in a crack house.

As a child, he assumed the position of the adult in the house and tried to help his mother, who was slowly killing herself with the drugs. He said that sometimes he was successful at convincing his mother to come back home to eat and to shower, but it was not always easy. He grew up around drug dealers, thieves, and thugs. He had no parental supervision. According to his testimony, he was 11 years old when his sister had a baby at 15. He said that he helped his sister with the baby as much as an 11-year-old could. It was only a matter of time before he did something that would either cause him to die or go to prison.

Brian Stevenson, the director of Equal Justice Initiative, said that even after the Supreme Court decided that sentencing juveniles to life in prison for crimes that are less than murder is illegal, some state courts were still very hostile to young children. Based on their actions, those officials do not care about the lives of the children and their potential to become important members of our society.

Children who are first, second, and third time offenders are, in the words of Bryan Stevenson, "demonized". We put them in a place to rot and die as if their future does not matter.

I totally agree with the Supreme Court's decision to eliminate the death penalty for juveniles. If they do not commit a murder, they should be given second chances, and they should be rehabilitated to serve their purpose in our society.

That is exactly what happened to Joseph in our biblical

story. He was removed from the free world based on a false accusation, and he was placed in jail for a while. Having served his time, he was released to accomplish what he was born to do. Prison did not keep him from the palace. Losing his freedom for a while did not keep him from serving the Egyptians and preserving them from starvation. If Joseph was rehabilitated and was able to save some lives, our incarcerated boys and girls should receive the same mercy when the crime of murder was not committed.

They must be given a second chance to go out in the free world and meet the needs of our community. We should not call them super predators, because, just like us, they were born to do something valuable in the world. Let us see them in all their potentiality, and let us give them an opportunity to exercise their gift and make our world a better place.

In both cases, Joseph and Kenneth were in prison for specific reasons. According to the Bible, Joseph did not touch Potiphar's wife, but he was, nonetheless, accused and put in jail innocently. Kenneth was also abandoned by his family; his father was never around to help him. He was forced to raise himself as a young child. Unlike Joseph, Kenneth did commit a crime, but he did not murder anyone. If Joseph was not given a second chance, the famine would have ravaged Egypt. Even the surrounding villages would have suffered had the criminal justice system in Egypt not given Joseph a second chance.

We must start looking at the background of those children that we are sending to death row, and we should try to help them reach their full potential so that they make our world a better place. We must always consider the reason for their crime before we sentence the next generation to hell.

Many children come from homes where they were abandoned and left by themselves. Like Joseph, they suffered at the hands of those who were supposed to protect and provide for them. It is so depressing that many of these children go from living in hell at home, then they transition to living in hades with hardcore criminals. Sadly, for those children, the pain never stops. Their only way out of this hell is death, unless we do something to keep them out of hell.

Every parent should embrace his or her life to protect children in general, and even to protect those that are left to raise themselves. We should have a little bit more compassion for our neighbors' children who may have a different background than ours.

According to the prison documentary of children in prison for life sentences, "African-American youth are sentenced to life without parole 10 times more often than their white peers." This simply means that there is a lack of compassion, and even a lack of willingness to help children who do not look like us. Let us make the world a better place for the poor children that are being tortured, neglected, prostituted, and coerced to commit violent crimes. Let us become merciful agents who change the world and take it from the villains who are terrorizing our children.

The story of Joseph teaches us that no matter the circumstances that shape our childhood, our destiny is set in stone. Everything that happened in the life of the young Joseph brought him closer to the fulfilment of his half-way revealed dreams. In the story, Joseph did not do anything intentional to bring about the realization of his dreams. He simply went through many hardships, and at one point in his life, what seemed to be nothing but disappointments. When the time was right, God helped him understand that his trials and tribulations paved the way for his success and the survival of His people.

If you were wondering how a wrongfully accused prisoner at Rikers Island, one of the worst prisons in America, can somehow embrace his or her life being caged like an animal, I can guarantee you that it is possible. If you were wondering how some of the modern-day slaves in Africa, the Americas, and all over the world could embrace their life, I want to propose to you that embracing life does not exclude tears and moments of despair. The great news is that, in due time, the tears will lead to the fulfilment of a purposeful life. The unimaginable cruelty and psychologically painful moments to which prisoners are exposed all over the world is quite depressing, but they are seasonal, because nothing lasts forever.

I know a man who has been in and out of the prison system since he was 13 years old. In fact, he always has a smile on his face even when we go visit him in prison. He has never hurt anyone physically, but he was a thief. His parents did not have much when he was a little boy, and as a kid, he stole to meet his needs. Because he did not kill anyone, I think that his sentences have been too harsh. It is heartbreaking to think of the life of a 13-year-old child in jail, regardless of what he or she has done.

There were speculations that the boy might have had mental issues. Unfortunately, he was never evaluated and given the proper help, because he had no one who cared enough to help him. God knows what he has gone through all these years in prison. As I write this book, he is scheduled to be released in a month. The sad fact is that he is bound to go back to jail if we cannot find a way to get him mentally evaluated. Furthermore, he will be released from jail with a warrant for an unpaid ticket. If they find him anywhere, they will arrest him again for the unpaid fine; it is a never-ending cycle.

His life stresses me out, because I want to help him, but I do not have the funds to do so. I do not know of any ministry that can help him in Huntsville. I believe that if I can get him the proper help, he will be a blessing at some capacity. It would not be surprising if he comes out of prison and becomes a mentor to young boys who could be on their way to a prison journey. Whatever happens at the end of his life, I know for a fact that it had a purpose. I might never know the purpose, but the Lord who made him will accomplish His will through him.

Chapter 10
How Do We Embrace Our Life?

How do we embrace our life? If we consider the story of Joseph with the limited amount of details available about the way in which he dealt with his brothers, we can see that Joseph simply lived his life, and everything happened naturally outside of his influence or manipulation. Joseph was meeting his brothers' needs when he was captured and kidnapped. His father sent him to go check on his brothers and to check on his flock. Joseph experienced hardships because he obeyed his father's command to check on the wellbeing of his brothers. Had Joseph not gone to serve his brothers, he would not have been kidnapped, he would not have lost the coat of many colors that his father made for him, and his brothers would not have conspired against him. Perhaps they might not have placed him in a pit, and they would not have sat and ate while Joseph was in a pit without water. Ultimately, they would not have sold him to slavery . . . at least on that day.

Meeting the needs of one another is guaranteed to usher us into our purpose, but it can also lead us into some dangerous situations. It can cause those whose needs we are meeting to envy us, and it can cause them to take our dignity from us. There is no guarantee that the people whom we are serving will appreciate and understand our service, nevertheless, we must continue to meet their needs.

How do we embrace our life in situations where we feel unappreciated for our service? We embrace our life by doing something in the community where we work; we do it to improve both our life and that of those around us, regardless if they appreciate us or not. We need not to be discouraged when embracing our life seems to only bring us loneliness, hopelessness, pain, and sometimes threats of death. We must press on and go do what we were born to do, not allowing any setback to discourage us from our purpose.

The Bible said that when Joseph got to Egypt, he was sold to Potiphar, who was an officer of Pharaoh and the captain of the guards. Although his family abandoned him, God was with Joseph so that everything he touched was blessed at the house of his master. Joseph met many needs upon his arrival in Egypt, therefore, the Lord prospered him, and his master put him over everything in his house, except his wife. While meeting the needs of his master, he was falsely accused and unjustly placed in prison.

While Joseph was in prison, there were two men, a baker and a butler; both had a dream on the same night. They both woke up confused and troubled about the content of their dream. One of the men, precisely the butler, told Joseph of his dream, and Joseph interpreted his vision. The butler was excited, because the meaning of the dream was favorable. Its meaning predicted that he was going to be restored into the service of the pharaoh. Joseph told the man to remember him when he was restored. He told the man to let Pharaoh know about his gift of interpretation and his innocence. The Bible said that the butler was indeed released from jail soon after, but he forgot completely about Joseph. Basically, he did not keep his promises, and Joseph remained in prison for a while longer.

When God has a plan for our life, people's attitude and behavior toward us does not discourage us. If it was up to people, we would never be promoted and we would never be set free. the Lord is the one who sets the captives free and who promotes our work in the community. Joseph's gift was forgotten until a real problem arose, and his expertise was needed. People might forget about your gift, but when the time comes and your services are needed, they will find you. God is able to arrange life's situation in your favor.

The second prisoner who had a dream had also asked

Joseph to help him with the interpretation. Unfortunately, the meaning of his dream was not as favorable as that of the butler. In fact, he was going to be put to death, which happened soon after Joseph interpreted his dream.

For a moment, it seemed as if Joseph's work in the prison went unnoticed. Despite a lack of immediate appreciation for his work, Joseph continued to meet the needs that arose in his jail community. The lesson is clear that if we meet the needs of those in our community, in due time, we will have a reputation, and we will be known for what we do in the community. However, there are obviously some needs that we should never meet.

We should never meet the needs of drug addicts by giving them liquid cash to purchase drugs. We should never meet the needs of individuals who want to establish their supremacy over their brothers. We should never meet unrighteous needs that can damage the community as opposed to benefit the community. We should stay away from meeting needs that divide families and cause children to have a horrible childhood experience.

Joseph was pressured by Potiphar's wife, who had a lustful sexual need that she wanted him to meet, but he refused, knowing that it would hurt more than it would help. Joseph got in trouble for refusing to meet a need that he knew could be devastating and could have serious consequences. He knew that meeting her sexual needs meant to offend his employer, and to sin against the God who was with him when his brothers kidnapped him. It meant to sin against the God who kept his brothers from killing him, to sin against the God who watched over him in the pit while his brothers were enjoying a great meal, to sin against the God who consoled his heart when he was depressed on the way to Egypt as a slave, and it meant to sin against the very God who prospered him in all that he did as a slave.

Joseph was too grateful to his God to allow a few minutes of forbidden pleasure to disrupt his relationship with the

Lord. He had too much respect for his master, and too much respect for the community to allow one selfish desire to disrupt the peace of the community. Consequently, Joseph ran and left his garment behind, escaping the seductive web of his master's wife.

The first time Joseph was caught by his garments, his brothers intended to hurt him, but God did not allow it. They were permitted to keep his coat of many colors, but the Lord delivered his body from their malevolent grip. Joseph was caught by his garment for a second time. This time Potiphar's wife caught Joseph by his garment, but she intended to use his body. Once again, the Lord delivered Joseph's body out of an evil grip, but He allowed Potiphar's wife to keep his garment. Sometimes, when we embrace our life, God will allow people to strip us of our status, but He will deliver our body. In both scenarios, Joseph's garments symbolized his distinctive identity and privilege among his peers. Joseph preferred to strip himself of his power and privilege so that he could maintain his relationship with his maker. Joseph was surely unhappy with both situations, nevertheless, he embraced his life.

Embracing our life does not mean that we should be happy with our situation, and it does not mean that we should pretend we do not have problems. In Genesis chapter 40 verse 15, Joseph complained that he was stolen away from the land of his family innocently, and he was placed in a dungeon for having done what was right. It is evident here that Joseph wanted his situation to improve. He wanted to get out of the dungeon even though he oversaw all the prisoners. Being a supervisor in a place where we are not supposed to be will certainly never bring us lasting joy. Being in charge, being blessed, and having a good social status while still a captive should not be our long-term goal. Being wealthy and loved by our community while our fellow brothers and sisters are poor, destitute and marginalized should not be satisfying to us.

We all should be free to exercise our gift, and to meet the

needs of those in our community as free men and women. Those who work for the Lord should not be captives forever, because the Bible said the Lord set the captives free. We should no longer be slaves, rather we should be placed in a position to improve our neighbors' lives.

While Joseph embraced his life and waited in prison for his opportunity to come, God created a situation to get His servant out of the unfortunate predicament in which Potiphar and his family placed him. When we embrace our life while trying to improve our situation, God will create different situations to get us out and free us for His glory and for our happiness.

Genesis chapter 47 verse 13-27 describes a severe famine that fell upon an entire region. It was so bad that both Egypt and Canaan were on the verge of annihilation, until the Egyptian authorities were told of Joseph's gifts. Embracing our life means to be ready to face the situation for which we were born.

I do not believe that God created the famine as the situation to get Joseph out, but I do believe that He created the baffling dream, and I believe that the Lord did not allow Pharaoh to understand its meaning on purpose. That is the situation that the Lord created so that Joseph could be set free, or maybe Joseph was created for that imminent situation. One man's dilemma is another man's opportunity for promotion, which means we were created for each other's benefit.

When Joseph appeared before the pharaoh, he was ready to start doing what the Lord embedded in his DNA to do. The pharaoh confessed to Joseph that he had a problem and he heard that Joseph was the only one who could solve it. Every need that we meet is recorded in the annals of the Lord. Every good deed that we have performed has been noticed by those around us. People may not sing our praises in our presence, but when the right time comes, at the opportune moment, in the presence of the right person, in the right social circles, and in the heat of the right moment, somebody will remember our work and will promote us in due time. Someone will think of the day that they were in trouble and we were the only ones who cared enough to meet their needs. A child will remember how safe and secure we made him or her feel.

Children who have grown to become adults and who now have a position of power will remember the goodness and the mercy we exercised toward them when they were vulnerable. Single mothers who begged and borrowed money to take care of their little ones will never forget that when they were financially stranded, and when they had nothing to feed their children, when they wept in secret for their lack of opportunities and financial resources . . . they will remember that we were the only ones who noticed that they were in trouble, and who lent to them that which they used to buy bread and clothes for their children.

Young men who were falsely accused, and who were on their way to prison, will never forget the faces and the goodness of the attorneys who did not defend their case because they were wealthy, rather defended them and gave them a second chance in life because it was the right thing to do. I have a friend from Florida who told me that were it not for a kindhearted white judge who gave him a second chance, he would have had a criminal record, and he would have probably spent his young life in and out of prison. Children will remember how they were treated in the past.

When I was a child, there was a young man named Jean-Claude who used to lend money to my mother. He was gracious, respectful, and patient to wait for my father to send us money so that my poor mother could repay him. He was a great friend to my uncle Wilfride, and he cared deeply about our wellbeing. I am forever grateful for this man who is now in Boston with his family. I have called him and thanked him for helping my mother when she was most vulnerable.

Joseph could take advantage of his opportunity, because

God made the butler remember what Joseph had done for him in prison. The need of the butler that Joseph met in prison affected the life of one person. The Lord gave Joseph another opportunity to meet a need that was on a greater scale. When Joseph met the need of the pharaoh, thousands of lives were affected. It is possible that the needs we are meeting right now in our community affect only a few individuals, but a time will come where the same needs that we are meeting now at a small scale, we will meet them on a greater scale to minister to more people.

Joseph was promoted from being a prisoner to being the pharaoh's second man in power. He was once Potiphar's second man in power, but God promoted him because he refused to meet the indecent need of his master's wife. Joseph made it from meeting the needs of his brothers in the field. He made it from meeting the needs of Potiphar's house. Joseph made it from meeting the needs of his prison community. He made it from meeting the needs of Pharaoh, and he finally made it from meeting the needs of his Hebrew family, placing them in the land of Goshen to care for them despite what they had done to him. He took care of them for the rest of his life. He was not revengeful toward them, but he took care of them unreservedly.

Conclusively, I ask how do we embrace our life? In a few words: we meet the needs of our immediate community.

Chapter 11
How I Embrace My Life in the United States

Fourteen to fifteen years after my father departed from Haiti and migrated to the United States of America, I became a man, having turned 21 in August 1996, two months after I was set to arrive in Miami. My father had submitted our paperwork to the US immigration office so that we could have a chance to come and reside with him in the US. We'd waited for a long time before we could finally, once again, live as a family.

In 1996, my father called my mother and told her that our files had been pulled, and that they were going to start working on our green card application. We were excited, but we knew that the process had just begun. We had to do bloodwork to make sure that we were related to each other, and that we were not going to carry any type of incurable disease to infect our new neighbors in the US. There were several different steps that we had to take before we could finally come to the US to live with Dad.

One day, my father came to Haiti and said that we had to appear before an officer of the US Embassy in Haiti for an interview and a final review of our papers, to determine if we were approved to receive a visa. I was excited, because I was finally going to be reunited with my father, and most importantly, we were going to be a family again. I cherished the idea that we were all going to live under the same roof as when I was a little child. This time, it was going to be better, because I was older and I looked forward to sharing with my father what we went through in his absence, and how much we missed him growing up.

When the day finally came for our visit at the embassy, my father, mother, and my two sisters and I all went bright and early to stand in line at the embassy. We waited for an hour or two before the American Embassy office was opened.

There were many people waiting in the line who did not have an appointment, but they were there to sell their spot in the line. That is how those people made money, for there were not any regulations to keep people from hustling one another while waiting for the embassy to officially open for business.

When they opened and we entered inside, it was a little bit more organized. We took a number and waited for our name to be called, after all, we had an appointment. When it was our turn to appear before the immigration officer, I was amazed and proud to hear my father speak in a different language, even though I did not understand anything he was saying. I kept saying quietly to myself, "Mezanmi, papa'm kòn pale anglè," which meant, "Oh my God, he knows how to speak English! That is amazing."

I only knew that it was English because I'd started learning English on my own in Haiti. I recognized a few words, but I had no idea what he was saying.

I was so proud of my dad, that when we got home from the embassy, I told him how I felt and how good I thought his English was.

"Anglè ou gen pou'l vin pi bon pase anglè'm." My father said to me that my English would be better than his English once I got to the United States of America. I did not believe my dad when he said that of my ability to speak the English language. It is not because I was intellectually challenged that I had a hard time believing my father, but it was because I thought his English was perfect. As my father predicted, my English is currently a little better than his. The proof is in my academic accomplishments, and in the faith that my father put in me to read his mail for him.

We were all granted a visa except my youngest sister Frandeline, which was odd, because most of the time the oldest child does not get approved for a visa. Therefore, I was both excited, but unhappy that my little sister was going to stay behind while Rodeline and I moved to the US. My mother said that she would stay with my little sister as much as possible, and she eventually received her own visa to come and be with the rest of us. After we were granted our visas, we left the American Embassy, and my dad went on to purchase our plane tickets. Oh, happy day!

Leaving Haiti, my sweet birthplace, was a bittersweet and unforgettable experience. On one hand, I was going to finally be with my father, and we were all going to live together and enjoy all the great benefits that came with living in Miami. As far as I knew, the US was the modern-day biblical land of milk and honey. On the other hand, I was deeply saddened by the fact that I was leaving people with whom I grew up; family members who knew me when I did not know myself. I was leaving behind Simone Antenor, who practically raised me and changed my diapers when I was but a small child. I was leaving behind Simone's daughter, Widline, whose birth brought a lot of light in my darkened childhood.

When Widline was a toddler, she called my mother "Mom," and she called her own mother "Simone." Liline, as we called her, was everyone's joy, just as my toddler Robyn is Pamela's and Trinity's joy in Huntsville. Pamela is my wife's sister, and trinity is her daughter. Robyn calls them both TT.

I wished there was a way for Liline to have traveled with us to the US, but a lack of money and economic influence prevented us from bringing her with us. I was going to leave behind my uncle Wilfride, who in the absence of my father, truly made me feel safe. And finally, I was leaving behind the relationships that I had created through the years. I was leaving Patrick, Jude, Fresnel, Moise, Domique, Matthieu, Fedline, Djoulie and Rose, who was a stepsister that I had just learned I had, and with whom I was just becoming acquainted.

I was sad and I was also happy, but I embraced my new life. I promised myself that I would one day go back to Haiti and help those whom I had left behind.

The time had finally arrived; my father, Rodeline, and I headed to the airport in Port-au-Prince. We went through security, showing our itinerary and our passports. As we waited to board our plane, for the first time in our life, my father had a serious heart-to-heart conversation with me and my little sister. I was already 20 years old, and Rodeline was 18 years of age. I have never forgotten what he said to us at the airport sitting on one of the benches as we listened intently.

"Etazini son gran peyi, men li se yon tè glise." What my father meant in English was that the United States was a great country, a place where one could thrive and become successful. "You will have the ability to go to school, and you might even receive financial aid to assist you while in school."

My father told us that the US was a great place to live for young people who aspire to become successful, but it was like a slippery slope. The same way you can become successful overnight or if you work hard, it is in the same way that you can fall in the United States of America. He said that you can end up in prison in the blink of an eye. My father spared me the scary details. He did not tell me that there was a possibility of being robbed, stabbed, arrested under false pretense, falsely accused, shot by thugs, or lynched by racist devils. He spared me the evil of drugs and addiction to alcohol. He spared me the evil of terrorist attacks.

I took my father's advice and kept it in my heart. Thus, I embraced a vision of making my father proud when I came to Miami. I cared deeply about what my parents thought of me.

When I arrived in Miami in June 1996, I was 20 years old, but I looked like I was 16. I did not know anything; I did not really understand the American culture. I did not have any friends, but none of that mattered, because I was in the US with my dad.

We never had a car in Haiti, but when we got to Miami, and after we retrieved our luggage from baggage claim, my father walked with us through a huge parking garage to his

1992 red Honda Accord. It was as if I was in a trance. His little four-door vehicle looked and smelled brand new.

The ride back to his small apartment in the outskirt of Little Haiti was pleasant. I watched with amazement the streetlights, the diverse passersby, the many restaurants, and the intertwined highways. I thought about my mother and my little sister who had stayed in Haiti along with Simone and Widline. They were most likely in the dark, because electricity was and still is scarce.

When we pulled up to the apartment, it must have been nine or ten o'clock at night. My father had a roommate named Frere Begel. He had been one of my father's coworkers in Haiti. He knew me when I was a little child, and he knew my family very well. In fact, I almost married one of his daughters. The old man was a kindhearted father and friend. He cooked us a delicious welcome-meal.

While my sister and I enjoyed Brother Begel's meal, we noticed that our father was getting dressed to leave the apartment. When we asked him where he was going, he said that he had to be at work. We spent the first night in the apartment with my father's roommate, and I was not too happy that he had to be at work all night, but I was pacified knowing that he would be home later.

We were not rich, but we were not dirt poor either. My father worked two jobs to support us financially. My sister and I were encouraged to go to school, in fact, we were registered at North Miami Dade High School to learn English. I embraced my life and did my best to learn the English language so that I could improve my condition of living in the United States, and one day return to Haiti to meet the needs of the many orphan children who pray every night for a helper.

I spent around three or four years in Miami learning and working on my assimilation in my new country of residence. After two years of ESL (English as a Second Language) courses to improve my English, I took it to the next level and

I decided to matriculate at the North Miami Dade community college. Meanwhile, I started serving at the Horeb Seventh-day Adventist church. I saw a need there to help with the youth, so I decided to make myself available to meet it.

I started helping at the church as much as possible, and made myself available in areas where I was needed. A few years later, having completed my degree in theology, I went back to the church and preached for a youth program. When I went back to Horeb to preach, I was living in Orlando, Florida, which was four hours away from the church's previous location. I did not really have the gas money to go preach on that day. In fact, my father gave me the money so that I could fulfil the preaching engagement.

I drove four hours to get to the church. After my service at the church, I was not given a dime or refunded the gas money that I used to come and serve the community. I did not ask them to pay me, because I wanted to give back to the church that received me when I first came to the US. Consequently, I was not upset and I did not make a big deal out of the situation. I embraced my life, even though I struggled to find the gas money to return to Orlando.

As a minister, I felt good that I'd offered my service to the community, and possibly saved the life of a young person.

In 1999, I left Miami and headed to Sarasota to live with Veronique, the friend who saved my father's life when he almost died in his car. My father was not too happy that I left Miami, but he respected my decision to move in search of a better life for myself and for the rest of my family. I felt that I was getting older and I needed to start contributing financially so that my aging father did not have to work as hard. My father felt that I decided to leave because I did not like his relationship with my mother.

When my mother came to the United States, and my sister Frandeline finally arrived, my parents started to argue about many unresolved past issues that occurred during the long and painful years they were apart from each other. They had bitter arguments and heated screaming matches. I was discouraged and very unhappy. I realized then that what I had envisioned as a perfect family reunion was never going to happen. There were times during their tantrums that I sided with my mother, and my dad knew it. I respected my father then, and I respect him now for having the ability to argue with my mother and restrain himself from ever harming her physically.

As my mother's son, as much as I love my dad, I do not think that I would be able to bear the sight of him physically abusing her. My father is not a perfect man, nor is my mother a perfect woman. I did not know that their relationship was rocky until we came to the US. That is when I embraced my life and decided that I had to leave the nest so that I could help them financially as they divorced each other.

I know that in the United States most children leave their parents' home at the age of 18 or 19, but in Haiti, children live with the family for as long as they want. It is partly because they have nothing else to do; nowhere else to go. But also, because they love to live together in one place.

I thought about enrolling in a truck driving school so that I could have a CDL license and be able to make some money. Consequently, I left Miami in search of a truck driving school. I spent a few months living with one of my father's old friends who had a son named Jeffrey. While living there, I was in constant communication with my father and mother back in Miami. I had also met a good Haitian friend at the Horeb Seventh-day Adventist church named Ronald Louis. He, too, had just come from Haiti, and we became good friends while attending the church.

Since Ronald cherished the same ethical and spiritual values that I held dear to my heart, we immediately connected and started to embrace our current situation. I worked hard to improve our life, our status of "boat people," and to fulfill our destiny in the United States. We were both helping at the church, because we both used to be very involved in our churches back in Haiti. That is why when I left Miami and temporarily stayed in Sarasota, I called Ronald and persuaded him to move with me to Orlando, Florida in search of a truck driving school, and ultimately to find a better life.

While living in Sarasota, I worked two to three jobs at several fast food restaurants, which enabled me to purchase a Chevy Sedan. I drove that Chevy back and forth between Miami and Sarasota. When Ronald agreed to move with me to Orlando, I went and picked him up from Miami, and we headed out on highway 75 to Orlando.

Once we arrived, we did not have friends and we did not know anyone in Orlando. We simply decided that we would move there by faith, and that we would find a Haitian Seventh-day Adventist church. We knew that if we found a Haitian church, we would eventually find a Haitian community. Thus, we were bound to find people who either knew us, or knew our parents.

We arrived there on a Wednesday night and decided to spend the night sleeping in my Chevy. We needed a parking lot that was well-lit for security reasons. We parked the car in the parking lot of a huge shopping plaza on the corner of Silver Star Road and Pine Hills Road. We locked our car doors and we prayed. We had our Bibles, and possibly our hymnals (I cannot recall precisely), out in the open, and I believe that I was pharisaical enough to kneel in the car as we prayed. It was very uncomfortable, but I was a naive and pious believer.

We were so innocent and such great believers that we closed our eyes and prayed as if we were in a secured house or temple. As we prayed with our eyes closed, we heard people around our car. When we opened our eyes, we saw several police officers with bright flashlights looking into the car with suspicion to see what we were doing. We rolled down the windows and we talked to them. They were surprisingly kind and helpful. They treated us with respect, and we explained to them why we were in the vehicle and what we were doing. They told us that someone called them and reported that there were suspicious activities in a gold Chevy parked in the parking lot of the Winn Dixie. We blessed the name of the Lord that we were protected on that night.

The next morning, we cleaned ourselves in public bathrooms and changed our clothes. Two days later, we rented a small apartment in the Rio Grande area of Orlando. From that point on, we met many Haitians, and I was even reconnected with some old childhood friends from Haiti. Schneider and Osselin, they were younger than me in Haiti, but we all used to play together at children's church. When my father moved to Florida in the 1980s, their parents moved to New York. We were separated for a while, but then reunited in Orlando.

Schneider and Osselin knew Orlando better than I did, therefore, they took me and Ronald under their wings and chaperoned us. We met them at the Guilgal Seventh-day Adventist church on Pine Hills Road during a lively worship service. Ronald and I were excited that we had connected with some people who were already established in Orlando. I also met one of my father's cousins who had two children, and was a member of the Guilgal Seventh-day Adventist church. She also looked out for us and helped us a little bit in Orlando until we could fly with our own wings.

Back in Miami, my mother told me that my father was sad that I'd left, and that they were all considering moving to Orlando to be close to me. That melted my heart, and I started looking for an apartment that could accommodate all of us. I embraced my life in Orlando and started working as a security officer. The idea and the plans to enroll in a truck driving school were obsolete on my mind. I decided, instead, that I would matriculate at the Valencia Community College in Orlando.

I must have spent a year there when I decided that I was not satisfied with my life and its trajectory. Consequently, I began praying and being more involved in the church. I joined a prayer group called "Étoile du matin." It was led by one of the greatest Haitian pastors in Orlando. His name was Ronald Jean-Baptiste. I was amazed by his vision for the Haitian church in the community, and I was attracted to the prayer initiative.

We met the spiritual needs of the community by visiting the members who were sick, and praying fervently with them. We used to have all-night prayers, seven-day prayer meetings, and 40-days of prayer. We even had a special prayer at five in the morning on Saturdays before our traditional worship service. We were on fire for the Lord, and motivated to help one another. I was dedicated to serve the Lord as well as the people of my community. I felt as though I was finally doing what I was called to do in life. Pastor Ronald Jean Baptist's religious and spiritual fervor helped me tremendously in my own journey. His charismatic sermons helped to spark in me the idea that I was born to meet a need.

As I worked in the churches in Orlando and served the community, I began to feel the need to do more and to serve at a greater capacity. I aspired to be like pastor Ronald Jean-Baptiste; to bring spiritual revival to an entire community.

I prayed and asked the Lord to guide me as I embarked on a new ministerial journey. I learned that in order for me to become a licensed pastor in the Seventh-day Adventist Church, and to be able to administratively serve the community, I had to attend a Seventh-day Adventist theological school.

I knew of several Adventist theological schools, but I preferred the then Oakwood College, and it had recently been renamed Oakwood University (OU). I chose Oakwood University for its famous reputation of preparing theologians who were skilled in preaching. I did not know how I was going to pay the tuition, because OU is a private HBCU with a high tuition cost. I clung to my faith and began to ask the Lord to help me find scholarships, and to help me be qualified for student loans so that I could be admitted. The Bible says that "faith without works is dead." Therefore, having prayed that the Lord make a way financially for me, I submitted my application to the admissions office, and I contacted the financial aid office to determine what my next step would be.

Having only four years of English language immersion, I did the best I could to gather the information needed to complete my application.

In the spring of 2001, I left Orlando, Florida and I traveled to Huntsville, Alabama. I left Orlando by faith; I did not know anyone in Huntsville, but I knew that I was going to school and was planning on living in the dorm. I had not received an acceptance letter from OU, and I did not have any proof that I was going to be approved for financial aid. I had told all my friends that I was leaving for college, and so they put together a going-away party for me. My guests did not know that I was leaving on faith. I kept that personal information from them, because I did not want them to discourage me from taking a leap of faith.

One of my great friends named Nirva gave me a nice blue Polo sweater as a going away gift, which made me very happy. I am forever grateful for her kindness.

I purchased a Greyhound bus ticket and left my parents and friends once again, but this time I left alone. My good friend Ronald stayed, but I took a bus and went to a school to which I had not yet been accepted. That was my efforts at improving my life and seeking better ways to improve the life of those around me.

When I arrived in Huntsville, I went to the school and met several Haitian students who were there for theology, business, nursing, education, and music. I also saw two young men who used to be members of one of the churches in Orlando. I immediately connected with them and stayed with them for a while until I could move into my dorm room.

The first time I went to the admissions office and inquired about the status of my application, I learned that some of my documents were misplaced, and that there was a possibility that I would not be accepted for admission that semester. I immediately left the office and went to the nearby restroom to pray. There I asked the Lord to create a way for me to be admitted to the school.

I went back to the office of admissions and met Miss Bowman, who was one of the women in charge of admissions. She patiently worked with me and registered me for school. I was admitted to OU on a conditional basis. I had to get all my documents in order, including either getting a high school diploma, GED, or a Haitian equivalent high school transcript.

The following semester, I opted to take a GED test to complete my application process. I successfully completed the examination and was awarded a certificate that satisfied my registration requirements at OU.

Prior to leaving Orlando, I prayed fervently and asked the Lord to bless me with a dorm room to myself. I did not want to have a roommate for the simple fact that I wanted to have my uninterrupted alone time with the Lord in prayer. It was foolishness to envision the possibility of having a private room when I was not yet admitted to the school. Moreover, first year students were never given a room to themselves in the dorm. I did not know the dean of the men's dorm at OU. I was simply going by faith, believing that I was going to be granted a private room according to my prayers.

Believe it or not, it was done according to my faith. The Lord worked it out so that my Pell Grant and my student loans came in at the right time. I learned while waiting in the long registration line that the private rooms at Peterson hall, which was the Freshmen dorm, only allowed student deans to occupy private dorm rooms. I did not allow this knowledge to weaken my faith, instead, I increased the frequency of my prayers and remained focused on obtaining a private dorm room against all odds.

They offered me several rooms, but I rejected them because I saw bunk beds, closets full of clothes, and shoes everywhere. I could not accept any of them because I did not want a roommate, and I believed with all my heart that the Lord was going to grant me a private dorm room.

I patiently waited on the Lord, and my faith was finally rewarded. One of the deans who was supposed to come for the spring semester decided that he would come in the fall instead. I was thus granted his private dorm room. To God be the glory!

The Lord kept providing for me throughout the school year as I clung to Him and to His Word. He helped me academically, He provided for me financially, He kept me out of trouble, and I eventually graduated from Oakwood University with both a bachelor's and a master's degree. I met many theology majors such as Johnson Cesar, Brian Ladiny, Ronald Michel, Daniel Brice, Wallace, Gerard, and many more students who used to meet in my private dorm room to sing and worship on Friday nights. We all embraced our life as students who came to prepare ourselves for ministry. We entered to learn how to minister, so that we could depart to serve and meet the needs of our community. I embraced my life in Huntsville, and gladly received my degree.

During my years at Oakwood University, I was invited to preach for several Haitian churches throughout the United States. I had left Orlando with the specific purpose of being trained in the art of preaching, pastoring, and ministering to the youth. Therefore, I was honored to receive several speaking requests, and to be able to stand before a crowd that varied between fifty to a thousand. I was blessed and felt like I was living my dream. I felt fulfilled because I was meeting needs.

My cup of joy and fulfillment overflowed when I received an invitation to go preach in Orlando at the church where my father was a deacon. It was the same church that Ronald and I visited when we first arrived in Orlando, and when we slept in the Chevy. I preached before an enormous amount of people. My father was in the crowd along with Frandeline and my mother. Rodeline was not in attendance because she was at

Andrews University completing her nursing degree.

After I charismatically delivered a sermon in English about the story of David and Goliath, my father came to me and hugged me. He told me in front of everybody that he was proud of me, and I could see it on his face and in his body language that he was truly proud to be my father.

As I basked in my father's pride, I remembered that he'd told me in Haiti, when I complimented him on his English after the interview at the American Embassy, that my ability to manipulate the English language would surpass his. I was also proud that thus far I'd brought a smile to his face, and not tears.

My father was not the only one who expressed his joy and satisfaction for my choice of work. My mother did not stop telling me that she was proud of me and that she loved me. In fact, she repeatedly sent me money while I was in the dorm. She was my best friend throughout my journey. She loved me and kept praying for me so that I wouldn't figuratively slip and fall in the United States of America. She prayed for my success and my protection. Thank God for a praying and loving mother.

The night that I graduated from Oakwood, I had a dream. I saw that I was climbing a steep and wet mountain. The mountain was high, and it appeared to be so scary that for fear of falling, I climbed it on my stomach. It felt like an eternity, but before the dream was over, I realized that while I was crawling on my stomach, there was a woman in front of me who was walking. We both got over the top of the mountain, and I got up from my stomach and started walking as well.

When I woke up the next morning, I knew that it was going to be hard for me to find stable employment. I understood that I was going to struggle financially for a while. The dream revealed to my heart that I was going to crawl to the very top of the mountain of success, but I was going to eventually get there. I believed in the Lord and decided to embrace my life and crawl as I worked hard at making it to the top. I remembered how back in Haiti the Lord had revealed to my mother her future, and how she came out of her situation victorious.

After receiving my bachelor's degree, I accepted a position at DirecTV as a CSR (customer service representative). The position had nothing to do with my degree, but I had to support myself financially, and it helped to pay my bills. I was not earning much money, but I was happy to start paying on some of the student loans. Although I did not remain there as an employee for too long, I was blessed to meet my best friend and wife, LaQueena, who had been with the company for at least eight years.

DirecTV had a policy that provided a full month of training for new hires. When I was in training, LaQueena was working on a special project for the company. She worked as a liaison between the customer retention group and managers to provide the best customer service, and to help retain both new and loyal customers.

When I laid eyes on her, I knew in my heart that I liked her. She was pretty, popular, bossy, jovial, and friendly. She was a godly woman who did not curse, and she carried herself as a virtuous woman who did not dress to satisfy the lustful predator's eyes.

She did not smoke, drink, party, or do drugs. I liked her and I decided that I had to make her my wife. I followed her with my eyes as she walked through the aisles of the call center handing out balloons and candy to encourage some of the frustrated CSRs. Part of her job duty was to take some of the representatives off the phone, and then schedule them to meet with her in her office for a one-on-one, relative to customer retention. I decided I would write something nice for her, using each letter of her first name. I waited for my opportunity to meet with her in her office to give it to her.

At the time, my supervisor's name was Jessica. She was an awesome supervisor who did her best to help her agents meet the company's goals. She worked with me and taught me how to serve the customers and to meet the required standards of the company. Jessica was strict and firm, but she was nice and did a great job with her team of workers. She was, at the time, a close colleague to LaQueena, and I thought that being one of her good agents would impress LaQueena if they both ever talked about me.

When we embrace our life and act as we are supposed to no matter what we are doing, people take notice of it and react to our attitude. Years after I left DirecTV, Jessica came to hear me preach several times.

I finally got time off the phone to meet with LaQueena. I was so excited about meeting with her and talking to her that I told Ronald about her. I knew that Ronald was annoyed with me, because I kept talking about LaQueena as if she was already my girlfriend. I was so crazy about her that I stored her name in my phone without her number. I promised Ronald that I was going to get her number, and that we were going to end up being together. I knew exactly what I was going to say to her. I planned to wait until I was sitting at her desk listening to what she had to share with me for my professional development, then at the very end of her presentation, I would make my move on her right there in her office.

I told her that I thought she was pretty, and that I had written something for her using the letters of her first name. It was quite embarrassing, but I did not care, because I truly liked her, and that was the best way I knew to attempt to show her that I was interested in her. I respectfully asked her if she would allow me to read to her that which I had written for her. I could tell that she was flooded with mixed emotion, because she was at work, and her boss was not sitting too far away.

As for me, no one else existed, and I had a mission to complete. I unfolded my little piece of paper and discreetly read it to her. I read it low enough to not get her in trouble, and she acted as professional as she could to give the impression that she was still doing a professional development meeting with me. She did not do anything wrong, she simply indulged her admirer.

After I read my acrostic poem to her, she kindly said that it was nice, but she also said that her little nephew, who was probably nine at the time, had recently done the same thing with the letters of her first name. I felt stupid and vulnerable, but I did not care about my pride at that moment. I was not discouraged after she told me that her nephew had done the same thing for her, in fact, I asked her for her number so that I could text the acrostic to her. She hurried up and gave it to me so that I would leave her office and get back to work.

I told Ronald that I had LaQueena's number, and a few weeks later, I introduced her to him as my girlfriend. While dating, we had several disputes, but we made it work. My parents loved LaQueena. They met her when I took her to visit them in Orlando. She and I became engaged after eight months of dating, and got married in Huntsville in the presence of our family members and our friends. Once again, my parents were proud of me for making such a life-changing decision.

I left DirecTV and enrolled at Drake State Community and Technical School to become a mechanic. I would have stayed with DirecTV had I found a schedule that allowed me to both work and continue with my education. Once again, I embraced my life and took a leap of faith in another direction.

My life with LaQueena was not perfect, but we embraced it as a married couple and met each other's needs as we grew in love. We both had a passion and love for service, and thus joined a little Haitian church in Huntsville. We gave it a few of our best years together.

I worked at Agape Haitian-American church with Pastor Wesley for over five years. I served there as an assistant pastor whose duties were to preach, teach, clean, visit the members, organize, structure, and plan worship services. I also worked with guest speakers, musicians, and the people in the community. Meanwhile, my wife served as the head of the children's church.

The children loved her and looked forward to going to church every Saturday knowing that Miss LaQueena would show them a good time. One of the boys who loved my wife's ministry at the church could not pronounce her name, so he called her Miss MaQueena.

During my ministry at Agape, I was blessed enough to have connected with many great people, and serve the community to the best of my abilities. I was honored when one of my good friends, Tracy, asked me to officiate her wedding with her now husband, Cameron. The more I embraced my life and served the community, the more I desired to serve and minister on a greater scale.

After a year at Drake State Community Technical School, I decided to quit for lack of money to purchase the tools needed to be a mechanic. I was not too happy dropping out of the program, because I loved what I was learning, but I needed the tools to practice. A man with a trade can never go hungry, but I could not continue with my trade.

My father raised me and provided for my every need because he had learned the trade of carpentry. My mother took care of herself when she was left all alone in the world and needed a place to stay and food to eat using the embroidery trade that she picked up when she was younger. I did not allow that miscalculation to discourage me and cause me to give up on myself and on my dreams. I kept looking for a better way to support myself financially, and to serve my community.

Things were tough at home financially. I worked to provide for our home while I pushed and supported my wife to finish her bachelor's degree. She, too, was forced to leave DirecTV as she focused on her education at the University of Alabama in Huntsville (UAH). We both left DirecTV in good standing, and were told that we would be able to come back if we ever had the need. I attempted several times to go back to

DirecTV, but on many of those occasions, I was told that they were not hiring.

My wife was not working and we had bills, so I accepted a position as a driver for Domino's Pizza, and I worked as a Walmart employee as well. I worked two full-time jobs and provided for both my wife and myself.

While I worked for those companies, I was still the acting assistant pastor at Agape. I served the community at church on Saturdays, sometimes going to the church early in the morning to open the doors and to pray for the service and the people who would be in attendance. Other times, I spent an entire day at the church. Most of my weekend time was spent working there to improve the life of the congregants, and to prepare for them a sanctified place of worship.

I remember one day working so hard at the church from six in the morning to seven at night. When I left the church, I headed straight home. My phone rang, and on the line was one of the young people from the church. She sounded worried and asked if I could come out and become a mediator between one of the married couples of the church who were having marital issues. I was tired physically and mentally; spiritually, I needed to be rejuvenated, but ministry was always my first priority.

I left my peaceful home and went in a war zone. When I arrived at the couple's apartment, the cops had already been called and a statement had already been taken. I counseled the couple as much as I could, and left the rest of it to the care of the Lord.

God was so good to me that He allowed me to prosper at both Walmart and at Domino's Pizza. I embraced my life and did my job at those companies with a smile on my face as much as possible. I was loved and respected. I did not complain about my jobs, but I kept working hard at changing my financial situation.

As I began to pray more about my finances and a better job, the Lord made a way out of no way for me. He had already shown me that I was going to crawl before I could walk. I did not know how long it was going to last, but I kept praying and working on myself. I decided to have seven days of prayer to ask God specifically to increase my income. Working for Walmart and Domino's paid the bills, but I had nothing left afterward to do any charitable work, or to take care of any of my wants.

My week of prayer was focused on asking the Lord to bless me with a new job. I asked the Lord specifically to help me find a job that paid at least $15 an hour. Walmart was barely paying me eight dollars an hour, and Domino's Pizza was a little less, because drivers receive tips as they make their deliveries. Fifteen dollars an hour seemed too high, even considering that DirecTV only paid $12 an hour.

After I completed a week of prayer in my prayer room, a week later my wife, who was a senior at UAH, came home from school and told me that one of her classmates had been bragging. My wife explained that her classmate claimed to have a daughter who was a manager at Appleton Learning in Huntsville. She was getting paid well, and was hiring people who were recommended to her. I reminded my wife that I was praying for a new job and that the woman might have the answer to my prayers.

The next day when my wife went back to school, she asked her classmate if she could help me get a job at her daughter's company. The woman gave my wife her daughter's information, and I was told to send my résumé to the company. My week of prayer was successful in the sense that the Lord answered my prayer affirmatively, and He gave me the desire of my heart.

The woman's daughter was in charge of recruiting teacher's aides for the company. I was hired, and my salary was exactly $15 an hour. It was done to me according to my faith. To God be the glory!

I worked for Appleton Learning for about two years. The Lord blessed me and prospered me at that company. I was so blessed and highly favored there that they hired any new recruits who mentioned my name as their reference. I was an aide for teachers who had special educational needs students in their classrooms; students who needed help with both the lessons and their behavioral challenges.

The job was tough. The children used to beat on me when their medications wore off. Some used to spit on me, while others called me names such as "Black African b*!@#." I had several who enjoyed running away from me so that I would have to chase them down the hall. Many times, I left the school with my shirt torn from a struggle to restrain students who became a danger to themselves and/or to the rest of the class. I did not get discouraged, because I was living and enjoying the result of my seven-day prayer. I gladly embraced my life, and embraced my new position as a teacher's aide to meet the needs of my special education students.

Believe it or not, I loved and enjoyed it, because the children had their special moments. One minute they loved me, and the next they called me all the unpleasant curse words in their foul, childish lexicon. I had to embrace it all!

While working for Appleton, I quit Walmart, but kept my position as a driver for Domino's Pizza. Once again, I felt the need to continue with my education, and to serve at a different capacity. I was still ministering at the Haitian church in Huntsville on the weekends, but I began to think about getting a second master's degree.

I considered many other things I could do to minister to children, as my experience at Appleton with the special education students birthed in me the idea to become a teacher who created a fun and an academic classroom environment for students to learn while playing. I prayed about it and asked the Lord to guide me in the process of finding the right school. I looked at several programs and several schools. I applied for both Vanderbilt and the University of Alabama. I was accepted at UA and I began a two-year French linguistics program there.

Having been accepted to begin a master's program at UA in the fall of 2013, I painfully gave my two week-notice at Appleton Learning, and regrettably explained to them that I was going back to school for at least two years, and it was out of town. My wife and I had talked about it, and we agreed to suffer for a while financially as I worked on improving myself academically, and preparing myself to minister at a higher level. We knew that it was not going to be easy, but we believed that the Lord would take care of us.

When I started the master's program at UA, I had a mortgage and a car note to take care of monthly, but because I was accepted on a full scholarship, I qualified for a $1,400 monthly stipend. It was certainly not a lot, but it paid our bills and allowed me to go to school tuition free. I prayed and worked hard at UA, and the Lord provided for my every need.

My first year at UA was hard, but the Lord kept me and helped me make it through. I traveled to Huntsville every weekend after my last class. Sometimes I was tired and drained from the rigorous academic labor in the program. It was intense and challenging. I had many papers to write, books to read, classes to teach, lessons to prepare, presentations to make, and papers to grade. When I got to Huntsville on the weekend, I had another load to carry. I had a sermon to preach, board meetings to attend, Bible study sessions, marriage counseling sessions, a worship service to coordinate, and sometimes members to visit.

At home, my wife wanted us to have date night, but I had no energy left. We argued and fussed sometimes, but we made it work. In fact, in my second year at UA, my wife and I decided to start trying to have a baby. We knew that we were not ready financially and that we were not stable enough to have a child, but I was getting older, and my wife was already in her 30s.

After five years of marriage, we began to seriously pray for a child. We actively worked to be fruitful and to multiply as we prayed for the Lord to bless us with a child. Our relationship with the children at Agape made us pray harder, and with more fervency for our own child.

At the Haitian church, I had my special kids who loved me and knew that I loved them as well. My wife also had her group of children who gave her a reason to want to have her own child. She had so many that I will only name a few. Isaiah and Giana loved my wife, whereas Josiah and Elayna were my favorite children in the whole world. I loved Josiah so much that when I was in town from school, I babysat him for free while his parents worked.

We continued to pray and to try to have a child for at least six months. My wife bought several pregnancy tests, but she was disappointed to see a negative sign as opposed to the anticipated positive sign.

Meanwhile, at UA, I had to complete the program within two years and maintain at least a B average to keep my scholarship. The Lord was truly good to me. I would have had a 4.0 GPA had I not taken two extra classes from a literature professor who was the personification of Satan on campus. The Lord was with me; He helped me to embrace my life in Tuscaloosa. He gave me the strength to endure the sarcasm and the blatant racism of that professor.

My journey at UA reminded me of the dream I had after graduation. I worked hard and truly crawled before I proudly walked with my Masters in French Linguistics.

In April 2015, the best year of my life, I was on Interstate 65 North when my wife called and told me that she had taken another pregnancy test. She was so delighted to see a positive sign that she could not wait for me to get home to share the great news with me. I was so excited and so shocked, I literally drove the car oblivious to anyone and anything around me until I made it to Huntsville. I kept thinking that I was going to be a father, and that my marriage with LaQueena had finally produced a tangible fruit. We were both elated and did not care if we had a boy or a girl.

When I arrived home, I held my wife's stomach and

attempted to talk to the embryo in her womb. We started taking pictures of her stomach, which was barely showing signs of pregnancy. We talked about possible names and the many great things that we wanted to do for our baby, who, as of this writing, is 22 months old.

After graduating from UA in May 2015, I went back home to Huntsville to my pregnant wife with no concrete promise of employment. I had spent some nights and days in prayer asking the Lord to make a way out of no way for me. I had prayed fervently for a teaching job after graduation, but upon leaving UA, I had not received a job offer. I had to go back to the prayer closet and ask God to speed the process, so that I could find a teaching position somewhere—anywhere—in the US. I wanted to have the opportunity to provide for my soon-to-be born child.

I remember hearing some of my classmates, while I was still at UA, talking about the many job offers they had received. I was not discouraged, rather I continued in prayer and waited on the Lord to find me employment. Although that summer was the toughest that I had experienced, I remained hopeful and believed that the same God who took care of me in Port-au-Prince Haiti, who provided for me in Miami, Sarasota, Orlando, Huntsville and Tuscaloosa, would provide for me again.

2015 was one of my best years in the United States. The summer was hard, but the rest of the year brought me nothing but joy and happiness. The Lord opened the windows of heaven and blessed us tremendously. I received a job offer from a private school in Virginia. They offered me the minimum that I wanted to start my teaching career. I was grateful to have found a school who wanted to hire me, and offered me the financial resources to provide for my family. I thought certainly that was the job that God had for me, because it came right on time.

I was excited and was ready to sign a teaching contract with the school. We had discussed and agreed on everything, when out of nowhere an email came in my inbox from a private school in Birmingham. The assistant principal was the angel that God had selected to bless me and my family for that special season of my life. I almost jeopardized the golden opportunity to work for one of the best private middle schools in the US.

I told the assistant principal that I had already received a job offer, and that I did not want to waste his time. I thank God that he ignored my comments and invited me to an interview at his prestigious school.

I was so impoverished that summer, I had to tell him I did not have the gas money to drive from Huntsville to Birmingham for the interview. He told me that if I could get there, he would reimburse me. I drove to Birmingham for the interview and saw the school. I looked at the pictures on the walls in the front entrance. I considered the administrative staff and said in my heart that they would never hire me because of my skin color.

My thoughts were based on the 16th Street Baptist Church bombing that happened on September 15, 1963 in Birmingham, where racist devils murdered four little black girls and injured several others. I thought this interview would be a waste of time, because people in Birmingham, Alabama did not like blacks.

I found out during the interview that I was wrong, based on the way the administrative staff welcomed me. They were professional and very kind. My interviewers were all very nice and courteous to me. We joked and laughed as they examined my credentials. I was wrong for assuming the worse about them, and after two and a half years, I have no complaints against any colleague at the school.

I was hired there and met many great selfless colleagues who mentored me and made me feel at home amongst them. Bo gave me his cellular phone number to call him if I ever needed anything. He, along with many others, have made me feel completely comfortable at this school. The parents were phenomenal. I never thought the private school family would treat me that good, simply because of the school geographical location.

The school was such a blessing to me that the admin staff worked with me and allowed me to finish a week of prayer that I was conducting in Florida for the youth at Église Adventiste Pergame. Chris Cadet, who was the youth director at the time, invited me to preach a weeklong back-to-school revival and spiritual renewal. It was such a blessing to minister to the church members in Florida.

The year 2015 did not only bring me a new job, a degree, and a speaking engagement in Florida, but it also brought me my citizenship and my first long-awaited fruit of the body, Robyn. I embraced my new life and welcomed new opportunities to serve my new community. I served at New Rising Star Church, and offered its youth a free of charge French Camp. I volunteered my time to pass out food, water, and clothes when the church had a program designed to bless 500 families in the community.

That was a short summary of the way I have tried to embrace my life in the US. I have not lived a perfect life, nor have I had the best assumptions of people, but I have always tried to serve and help those in need around me.

If I am successful with this book, and if you would help me to pass it on, I will reach and encourage all kinds of people that would probably never meet me in person. I have tried my best to encourage you to use your past situations as well as your current ones for your benefit and that of others. Embracing my life in America, and always seeking to improve it, has led me to write this book, and I pray that it has already blessed your spirit.

Ronald, one of my best friends

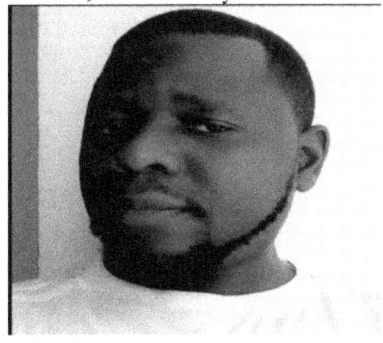

Epilogue
EMBRACE YOUR LIFE!

It is a well-known fact that we did not all have a glorious and happy childhood. Consequently, most of us choose to keep our childhood, or certain experiences in our childhood, a secret from our life partner, colleagues, and our social media friends. In this book, I explicated my rationale for teaching others to embrace their life no matter their circumstances. That was my true purpose in sharing the many personal stories and my research-based reflection on childhood experiences around the world.

I found it fascinating that most successful people, not referring to net worth here, had a challenging childhood, yet they have embraced their life and have become some of the most successful people in the world. The previous chapters are replete with examples of such people. They have overcome unsurmountable difficulties by embracing their life. It benefited them as opposed to hurting them. They knew that none of us had any control over the life that we have received from the Creator, and the experiences we have had in our childhood. In fact, they may not have ever reflected on the rationale for embracing their life, but based on their successes, I can infer that they understood it was a better alternative.

This book is proof enough that I agree with the idea of embracing one's life, for I understand clearly that there may not be a difference between us human beings and a manufactured transportation vehicle. I see startling similarities between me, a car, an airplane, a motorcycle, a bicycle, or anything that was purposefully manufactured. I see a deep comparison between humans not having a choice in their birth place, birthday, and family members. I see vehicles made to transport people or things, not having a choice in their assembly location, or a choice in their prospective owners.

It is benefiting to reflect on the fact that neither humans nor transportation vehicles had the option to agree or disagree prior to being born or manufactured. A higher being--or a higher consciousness–has manipulative control over the matter decided through research, trial, error, and pilot studies to assemble a car capable of meeting our common transportation needs as humans. Similarly, a higher being that created the maker of our vehicles put a human being together with a body, soul, and spirit.

According to the History Channel, the first steam-powered road vehicle was built in 1769 by a French military engineer named Nicolas-Joseph Cugnot. It was a tricycle made for the purpose of hauling artillery. It could run for 15 minutes and was only able to go as fast as 2.25 miles per hour. For obvious reasons, Nicolas-Joseph did not consult with the first vehicle he made, and he did not get a signed consent from the tricycle that only existed in his mind in the form of an idea. It would have been totally impossible for that conversation or for an agreement between a car that only existed in the mind of its maker to have occurred, for the simple fact that Nicolas's invention was not aware of its maker.

Obviously, devoid of consciousness, a car cannot communicate intellectually with its manufacturer. I find the same deductive reasoning to be true for us human beings. Common sense says that we did not make ourselves. We were not aware of our Creator, because we lacked the consciousness and intellect, prior to receiving the breath of life, to have the opportunity to agree or disagree on the location and the purpose of our birth. A higher consciousness through great wisdom must be responsible for our existence in the physical form. If that is the case, the higher consciousness must have had a purpose for our life. The idea of our existence must have been in the thought world before it materialized itself, through the machination of a manufacturer, in the physical world.

I am beyond grateful for Nicolas's invention. While I teach in Birmingham during the week, it allows me to see my family, who lives in Huntsville, every weekend. His invention makes my life a little better, and it brings a lot of joy to my daughter Robyn, who is always happy to see me at the end of a long week of work and labor.

The first vehicle was made to haul artilleries in the French army. Its construction was planned for a specific purpose. The vehicle did not choose its purpose, instead, its maker built it with a purpose in his creative mind. Every part of the vehicle was designed to serve a purpose. From the windshield to the thread on the tires, everything in the vehicle was purposed to meet a need. Great care and lots of research helped to assemble the car. I see great parallels in the way we as humans were shaped and formed in our mother's womb.

My pretty wife, LaQueena, is currently six months pregnant with our second daughter, Layla Love. Layla is being assembled like a vehicle in a well-equipped womb, designed to prepare her for her purpose in the outside world. The conscious wisdom that is constructing and fashioning my precious Layla takes great care to strategically build us to meet a need. Every part of Layla's body serves a purpose. From her head that housed her brain, to her feet that transport her body, every part is being assembled for a purpose.

After assembly, a vehicle is usually sold to meet the need of individuals who may want either a larger car, smaller car, sports car, or a luxury car. One may agree with me that we were made for a purpose, but may still argue that there is no comparison between humans and a vehicle made to transport them. They may bring "free will" into the conversation and argue that our manufacturer made us with the power to choose. Whereas a car is not conscious to choose who will own it, or whether it will serve its owner or not. That is true to a certain extent, except that just as a car cannot operate without a human being controlling it, the human body cannot operate without something outside of it such as its life force.

The body is, indeed, a transportation vehicle for the soul and spirit of every human. Without it, we cannot exist in the physical form, and therefore cannot be on the highways and underpasses of the material world. We need a body to be part of this world just as the fish need a body to be part of the oceanic world. The interesting fact is that we did not know that we needed a body until we became aware of ourselves. Our fate and purpose were decided for us before we became aware that we were in a state of oblivion.

At first, none of us knew why we were manufactured. Just as a child waking up from a long nap takes time to recognize where he or she is, it takes us a while after birth to realize where we are and why we are there. Most of the time, even the family that birthed us do not know our destiny. It even takes time for family members who raised us to recognize and acknowledge the purpose of our birth.

Such was the case of Jacob, the father of Joseph. He had no idea that one of his sons, little Joseph, was born to be an important leader in Egypt, and that he would one day be the savior of his generation. Whatever hope and aspirations Jacob had for Joseph expired when his other children told him that Joseph died a horrible death. As a father, living with the knowledge that one of your sons was torn apart by wild beasts and died in a state of excruciating pain and helplessness would be miserably pointless. Little did Jacob know, l'homme propose mais Dieu dispose. God had manufactured Joseph for a purpose, therefore, Joseph could not die until he served his purpose.

We must embrace the life for which the manufacturer built us. We must play our part in the fate of humanity. If each one of us fulfils his or her purpose, the world will no longer be a dysfunctional place. You have a special role and an important mission in this world. Do not allow your past or your current situation to deter you from what you were built to do. Embrace your life no matter what, or both you and the world will suffer the consequences.

First, you will go through life bitter, and you will possibly be hateful toward the people who love you the most. Second, the world will suffer because no other human being can play your role as well as you can.

A soccer team that wants to win a final game tries its best to avoid a red card. The reason being, a red card will cause the team to play the rest of the game with one less player, and will ultimately place the team in danger of losing the competition. If we do not embrace our life and make the best of it until we are naturally ushered into our destiny, we will cause the human team to experience the game of life at a disadvantage. We embrace our life when we play our position and strive to not bring a red card to the team. Simply deciding to go about your day looking and being happy may bring you real joy and bring someone else some happiness. Allow me to preach for 10 seconds as I cannot resist the urge . . .

Embrace your life as a divorced man or woman! Embrace your life as a single parent! Embrace your life as an adopted child! Embrace your life as a blind man or woman! Embrace your life as a recovering addict! Embrace your life as a police officer! Embrace your life as an activist! Embrace your life as a felon! Embrace your life as a victim of deportation! Embrace your life as a victim of racial attacks! Embrace your life as an orphan! Embrace your life even if you have never met your biological father or mother! Embrace your poor life and embrace your wealthy life! Embrace your single life! Embrace your married life! Embrace your life of pain and suffering! Embrace your life with troublesome children, and embrace your life with many miscarriages! Embrace your life as a veteran! Embrace it all, for your life has a hidden purpose.

I embrace my life as a French teacher for the moment, until my Maker shows me another way to serve the world and meet a need. Embrace your life no matter your current or past circumstances. Sooner or later you will do what you were born to do.

Many of us have been trying to figure out our purpose, and are still confused as to what we are supposed to do or what need we are supposed to meet. As a child, I thought that everyone discovers their purpose in life when they are older. Unfortunately, I found out that even older people can sometimes go through life and never discover their purpose. The problem is that some of us might have already fulfilled part of our main purpose unknowingly. The following account, the last story that I will use to conclude this book, testifies to the reality that many of us serve our purpose unknowingly, and at an early stage of our life.

The story of Ruby Bridges (the first little girl to attend the all-white William Frantz Elementary school in 1960 during the American desegregation era in Louisiana) confirms that we sometimes fulfil our purpose without any knowledge of our personal mission in life. Ruby's childhood was legendary in terms of what she endured in the South. She was only six years old when her parents volunteered her to be the first child who matriculated at an all-white school in the South. I probably would have never done this to my little girls, but if that was their purpose in life, I would not be able to prevent it from happening.

When I first read the story and watched the movie, I asked myself how the precious six-year-old Ruby could go to a school where no one liked her and no one accepted her. I was angry with the parents who put her through such a horrific and torturous childhood nightmare. I could not understand the rationale behind sacrificing the innocence of a little girl for the sake of integration, which led to the destruction of the black economy. I imagine how lonely she must have felt walking the halls of the school . . . the indifference and rejection she must have experienced from students who looked nothing like her. I even wondered how and where she ate her school lunch, with whom she played and talked, and how she could learn while living in such a dysfunctional, diabolical, and hateful society.

Like my current students at school, Ruby found a way to mask and hide her unpleasant situation. She probably came up with a system to help her sleep at night, deal with her nightmares, and function in a schizophrenic white supremacist culture during the day. Although she was only a six-year-old, she learned to ignore the constant barking and mauling of the evil men and women who traumatized her with their insensitive, rude, ignorant, barbaric, and racist comments and gesticulations.

I understand now that Ruby Bridges was born to be the sacrificial lamb who desegregated the schools in the South. She was born for it even if she was not aware of it at the time, but the Creator gave her life for that purpose.

Embracing her life every day meant that she had to endure the same barbarism for years, not in a jungle in Africa, but in one of the acclaimed "civilized" nations of the world. I am honored to write this portion of the book on her birthday. Ruby Bridges was born on September 8, 1954. Today, as I write this paragraph, she turned 63 years of age, and she looks healthy and beautiful, as if she had a perfect childhood. I believe that she made her contributions to society and had an extraordinary childhood. Her childhood was sacrificed so that I, a black man from Haiti, could have an opportunity to work at a white private school in the deep south, Birmingham, Alabama.

We do not choose our purpose in life. Each one of us is born with a mission in our DNA. Therefore, we must embrace any and every situation in which we find ourselves. We never know which situation we were born to handle, which problem we were born to fix, which book we were born to write, which disease we were born to cure, or which human puzzle we were born to solve. The bottom line is that we need to embrace every facet of our life and be proud to meet the need of our fellow brothers and sisters of every race and every ethnic group. The children of the world are counting on us to embrace our life and make the world a better place for them. Will you join me as I embrace my life, by embracing your own?

Prayer

Creator of all things, I pray that you bless everyone who took the time to read this book. Show them practical ways to embrace their life and meet the specific needs for which you created them to meet. Give to each reader the strength to endure their life's challenges.

I pray for the many children all over the world whose childhood is a nightmare. Please strengthen their innate abilities to withstand the abuse and neglect to which we adults expose them. Give them the help they need to embrace their life.

I pray for our prisoners living in a hell that we have created here on earth to punish their mistakes and crimes. Lord, I pray for the single mothers raising children without any financial help, and living in places that are not safe for their children. I pray for my students, and students in general throughout the world, who have a hard time at school. Please protect them from their evil tormentors both at home and in the school yard.

I pray for our world leaders and their weapons of mass destruction. Please help them to consider using their weapons and their money to create a safer world, not just for their children, but for all children living in the four corners of the world.

I pray that the content of this book ignites a strong desire of each reader to brainstorm ways to improve the quality of life for children in their community and beyond. I pray that this book melts the heart of those who are selfish, and turns them into philanthropists who compete to change the world one child at the time. I pray that you turn millennials into a generation of children who gives, who loves, who protects, and who revolutionizes the world, and causes previous generations to wonder at their children's benevolent proclivities. I pray that this book is a blessing to me and my readers.

Amen!

About the Author

Born and raised in Port-au-Prince Haiti, Robins Compere moved to Miami, Florida in June 1996, where he resided for five years. There he took ESL courses at North Miami public high school. He then moved to Orlando, Florida, where he worked on behalf of the youth at several Haitian churches in the Pine Hills area. In the spring of 2001, he relocated to Huntsville, Alabama and enrolled at Oakwood University as a theology and French student.

During his studies at Oakwood, Robins went to France as an exchange student to complete his bachelor's degree in French. He remained in Huntsville and completed a master's degree in pastoral studies.

In 2013, Robins matriculated at the University of Alabama, and graduated in 2015 with a master's degree in Romance Languages, with a concentration in French Linguistics. It was a blessing for Monsieur Compere to have joined an esteemed private school's team in 2015, and to still be a proud member today.

Robins is a proud father of two beautiful girls, Robyn and Layla, and he is happily married to his queen, LaQueena.

Resources

Vezina, Renee A. "Combating impunity in Haiti: Why the ICC should prosecute sexual abuse by UN peacekeepers." (2012).

Grady, Kate. "Sexual exploitation and abuse by UN peacekeepers: A threat to impartiality." International Peacekeeping 17.2 (2010): 215-228.

Faedi, Benedetta. "The double weakness of girls: Discrimination and sexual violence in Haiti." Stan. J. Int'l L. 44 (2008): 147.

Aristide, Jean-Bertrand, and Amy Wilentz. *In the parish of the poor: Writings from Haiti.* Orbis Books, 1990.

Hallward, Peter. Damming the flood: Haiti, Aristide, and the politics of containment. Verso, 2007.

Aristide, Jean-Bertrand. Eyes of the Heart: Seeking a Path for the Poor in the Age of Globalization. Common Courage Press, 2000.

Louverture, Toussaint, and Jean-Bertrand Aristide. The Haitian Revolution. Verso, 2008.

Aristide, Jean-Bertrand. Dignity. University of Virginia Press, 1996.

Dupuy, Alex. The prophet and power: Jean-Bertrand Aristide, the international community, and Haiti. Rowman & Littlefield Publishers, 2006.

Oppenheimer, David Benjamin. "Martin Luther King, Walker v. City of Birmingham, and the Letter from Birmingham Jail." UC Davis L. Rev.26 (1992): 791.

Smith, Petric J. Long Time Coming: An Insider's Story of the Birmingham Church Bombing that Rocked the World. Crane Hill Publishers, 1994.

Sikora, Frank. Until justice rolls down: the Birmingham Church bombing case. Fire Ant Books, 2005.

Wagner, Laura Rose. When the one who bears the scars is the one who strikes the blow: History, human rights, and Haiti's restavèks. Diss. The University of North Carolina at Chapel Hill, 2008.

Dieperink, K. B., et al. "Embracing life after prostate cancer. A male perspective on treatment and rehabilitation." European journal of cancer care 22.4 (2013): 549-558.

Finkelstein, Norma, and Laurie S. Markoff. "The women embracing life and living (WELL) project: Using the relational model to develop integrated systems of care for women with alcohol/drug use and mental health disorders with histories of violence." Alcoholism Treatment Quarterly 22.3-4 (2005): 63-80.

Boler, Tania, and Kate Carroll. "Addressing the educational needs of orphans and vulnerable children." (2003).

Alang, Sirry, et al. "Police brutality and black health: setting the agenda for public health scholars." American journal of public health107.5 (2017): 662-665.

Koch, Fiona. "James Jones' unarmed black male: exploring human stories behind the numbers of police brutality." POLIS: journalism and society at the LSE (2017).

Bender, Mariah. "Black Lives Matter: Reflections on Ferguson and Creating Safe Spaces for Black Students." Critical Education 8.2 (2017).

Allenby, Rebecca, et al. "Safety in online research with women experiencing intimate partner violence: what about the children?" Ethics & Behavior 27.1 (2017): 26-42.

Rosen, Lisa H., Kathy DeOrnellas, and Shannon R. Scott. BULLYING IN SCHOOL. PALGRAVE MACMILLAN, 2017.

Straus, Murray A., Richard J. Gelles, and Suzanne K. Steinmetz. Behind closed doors: Violence in the American family. Routledge, 2017.

Bonilla-Silva, Eduardo. Racism without racists: Color-blind racism and the persistence of racial inequality in

America. Rowman & Littlefield, 2017.

Taylor, Melanie. "USA." International Handbook of Juvenile Justice. Springer International Publishing, 2017. 135-152.

Gongola, Jennifer, Daniel A. Krauss, and Nicholas Scurich. "Life without parole for juvenile offenders: Public sentiments." Psychology, public policy, and law 23.1 (2017): 96.

Dillon, Mary E. "Juvenile Justice and Adolescent Health: Crime, Punishment, and Life-Course Trajectory." International Handbook on Adolescent Health and Development. Springer International Publishing, 2017. 241-265.

Lehmann, Peter S., Ted Chiricos, and William D. Bales. "Juveniles on Trial: Mode of Conviction and the Adult Court Sentencing of Transferred Juveniles." Crime & Delinquency (2017): 0011128717714203.

www.ingramcontent.com/pod-product-compliance
Lightning Source LLC
Chambersburg PA
CBHW031630160426
43196CB00006B/348